MEMOIR
OF A
Chihuahua
BAT

Susan Stanford

outskirts
press

Outskirts Press, Inc.
http://www.outskirtspress.com

Paperback ISBN: 978-1-9772-1358-7
Hardback ISBN: 978-1-9772-1360-0

PRINTED IN THE UNITED STATES OF AMERICA

Notes from the Author

This book is my recollection of events that I have related to the best of my knowledge. All names and identities have been changed or are composites. Some events have been compressed and some dialogues were recreated.

Edited by Eve Holmans Raine Thank you for your creative insight into the world of public education.

If anyone had ever told me that I would find myself in such an unbelievable teaching environment; honestly I would not have believed it. As unpleasant as the day to day struggles were, this test challenged me to grow and become a better teacher. My wish for all educators is this: I hope you find, your Mala, that person that inspires you to be better and makes you laugh. That is worth more than a paycheck.

Mala and I spent five years together at North Gate High School. During those five years we created twenty-two instructional books about best practices in the Foreign Language classroom, developed eight different presentations, and formed a company The Chihuahua Bat. In 1999 my husband was transferred out of state. No longer at North Gate, Mala and I continued to develop products for our company. In fact, being at different schools gave us a broader perspective of the public classroom and enabled us to reach more educators. We had one rule as consultants: Never leave the classroom. We gained respect from our audiences because we were walking in their shoes and could honestly address their concerns.

Many have asked: Where are the Bats now? Mala and I, now retired, still gather, reflect, and collaborate. Yes, we are still flying around the state causing trouble. You will find us drinking coffee on the front porch of her El Ranchito or enjoying wine on the bank of the river in front of her cabin. We still advocate for teachers in the classroom on our website, chihuahuabat.com. So check out our blogs and dare to become a Chihuahua Bat.

DEDICATION

For Mala

Table of Contents

Acknowledgements

To my family, Mike, Taylor, Chris, and Kate,

I am so grateful for all your, love, understanding, patience, and support during my career and this project. You all began the Chihuahua Bat journey with me and know firsthand the sacrifices that we all made. Your encouragement and advice helped me stay the course. Thank you for all the memories.

To Cherryl, my Chibat partner in crime. I am thankful that you answered the phone on that hot July day in 1993 and took a chance on me. You brought out my best when I was faced with a challenging teaching situation. Working with you were the best educational years of my life. Thank you. During our first conversation when we shared our experiences, I knew that we were destined to change the world. And we did!

A giant thanks to Bob and Mike, who chose to reconcile our checkbooks and receipts, edit our books and materials; hike through México year after year with our students; support our massive Market, Restaurant, Museum, and Fería projects; and chose to nurture us as we evolved into the Chihuahua Bats. Most of all, thank you Binko (Bob) and Bat Flash (Mike) for being Chihuahua Bat Husbands.

To Eve, thank you for helping me find my words and develop my thoughts. You took me from words on a page to a neatly stitched three-dimensional story. I am forever grateful for all the endless hours you devoted to my project. Having walked in the shoes of a teacher, you understood the struggles we faced every day in the classroom.

Thank you to my Breakfast Club colleagues who lovingly supported Mala and me and what we stood for in the classroom. That ten minutes of coffee and conversation in the mornings was just the attitude adjustment I needed to survive the Industrial Arts room. Thank you! The Breakfast Club Got it!

To Gloria, thank you for encouraging me to tell my story.

Preface

To all of my educational colleagues—whether you are a new teacher or a veteran; whether you are beginning a new academic year or are already deep in the throes of one; or whether you are on a brief holiday respite (but probably still having to work because a teacher's work can be 24/7/365)—I am thinking of you. If your school year is just beginning, you are perhaps wearing the new district T-shirt with that inspirational motto for the year, and you are surely being greeted with enthusiasm and optimism as you await the arrival of your students. A new year will bring changes in personnel, policies, and procedures, but that can also happen at any time (as every veteran teacher knows). However, at some point, you will have settled into your routine.

You might be sailing along, albeit in occasional choppy waters (for weeks or even for months), but then, the unforeseen happens. At any given point in a school year, the powers that be might change something that would alter your established comfort zone. How do you react? You may wish that you could just get out of that boat, but certainly, you need to stay in the boat and keep paddling forward. Once in awhile, though, you may just need to rock that boat.

My wish is that you have a great year with great students and great learning results. However, if you find yourself struggling with teaching content or managing your student population or any number of other myriad issues, here is the secret: Success has to come from you.

Perfect conference periods, perfect curricular products, and perfect students do not exist. Moreover, don't count on your administrators to calm the waves of your rough waters; they have their own issues to solve. Plenty of road-block opposition will come your way, and it can come from all corners of a campus—from administrators, from other colleagues, from parents, and from the community at large. Any and all might tell you (as they had told me over the course of my twenty-nine-year teaching career), what can and cannot, should and should not, be done as the teacher in charge of your own classroom—your little corner of the world.

Thus, to the new or the veteran teacher, if you are feeling discouraged—at the start of a year or in the midst of one—may I encourage you to read my story? Memoir of a Chihuahua Bat will entertain, inspire, and encourage you. My story starts with me arriving at a new school district after ten years of serving elsewhere in the public classroom.

I am anxious and nervous to start over again in an unfamiliar setting—that is, until I meet Mala, my new colleague and soon-to-become 'partner in crime' and fellow Chihuahua Bat. Come along as I retrace my steps on one part of my journey as an educator—and a crazy, roller-coaster ride of a journey it was! Then, upon its conclusion, ask yourself the question that I hope will become a memorable and inspiring one for you: "What would a 'Chihuahua Bat' do?"

A successful teacher loves his or her subject and is passionate about teaching it to others. Unleash your enthusiasm. Go beyond the textbook; go beyond the standardized, federally and state-mandated tests; instead, show your students how to love learning. Remember: In the end, success is up to you. To that end, don't be afraid to rock the boat. Dare to be a Chihuahua Bat.

Introduction

In 1993, two complete strangers met over the phone; shared their passion for teaching; and formed the Foreign Language Department for a small school district in South Texas. Commonly, they were each married mothers of three. They were each experienced Spanish teachers. They each had followed their husbands, whose careers had taken them from city to city.

I remember the first time I ever heard Mala's voice and thinking, *This school is going to be an adventure.* She was comical, witty, and uncensored. I never knew what was going to come out of her mouth. By contrast, I was poised, professional, and polite. As a team, we were perfect. She provided the one-liners, and I provided the diplomacy. This is our story.

ONE

Sometimes, It's Good to Work for Idiots

I had received a tip from a friend of a friend about a teaching position at a local high school. You see, my husband had accepted a position in South Texas, so I was looking for a job. I nervously dialed the phone number and asked to speak to the high school principal. The male voice cleared his throat three times and hesitated as he falteringly tried to answer my questions. "This is the middle school principal—I mean the high school principal—can I help you?"

"Yes, I am calling about your Spanish position. Has it been filled?"

"Well, I'm not sure; just a minute; hold on." Suddenly, I was listening to dead air. A few seconds later, he returned. "I think it's still open."

"Great! I would like to interview for this position. Are you still scheduling interviews?"

"Well, I am not sure. Just a minute please."

Once again, I found myself on hold and looking at the receiver in disbelief. *What kind of principal*, I wondered, *cannot answer questions about a position at his own school?* He returned, apologized, and asked for my name and phone number and said he would call me back and let me know if they were still interviewing for the position. As I hung up the receiver, I remember thinking, *This is the strangest conversation that I have ever had with a principal. What have I gotten myself into?*

I immediately called my husband. "There is no way I can work for that principal. I'm sorry, but he is an idiot. He could not answer any of my questions. He couldn't even tell me if the position had been filled, or if he was still interviewing. I'm telling you he is an idiot!"

"Swan, before you jump to conclusions, let's give this man the benefit of the doubt. You don't know what he is dealing with."

"Okay, but I have a weird feeling about this."

Three hours later I found myself sitting in the idiot's office waiting for an interview. I watched as all kinds of people came in and out of the administrative office. Being a 102-degree hot day in South Texas, everyone entering the office made a comment about the heat. The parents of the athletes were concerned about the afternoon practice; the groundskeepers were concerned about watering restrictions and the condition of the football field; and the custodians were upset about cleaning the buildings with the air conditioning being turned off in all buildings except one. Since, during summer months, the administration building was the only air-conditioned building on campus, people found numerous reasons to enjoy a few minutes in the cool air.

At 1:20 p.m., I heard a voice say, "Hello, are you here for the Spanish position?" I looked up to see a tall, tanned, blonde-haired man wearing gray athletic shorts, a gray football T-shirt, and athletic shoes. The look on my face invited his next comment. "Not only am I the principal, but I am also the varsity football coach. Please excuse my attire; I have practice today after our interview. My name is John James. Please, come in, and I'm sorry about the wait. I'm the only one in the office this week. My secretary had an emergency today, so I am quickly learning how to work the phones."

Okay, I thought, *that accounts for the first set of 'well-I-don't-knows.'*

He proceeded to explain that, typically, I would interview with him and then immediately afterwards I would talk with the department chair. Today, however, as he continued to explain, the department chair was unable to come in to interview me in person. Thus, I would be having a phone interview with her. Talking with Varsity Coach/Principal James was professional and consisted of my answering a series of questions, followed by a tour of the campus, which consisted of five buildings. Mr. James led me in a quick walk-through of these, calling each by its name: Administration Building, Athletic Building, Fine Arts Building, High School Building, and Middle School Building. We then returned to his office, and he called the department chair, Jean Smith, to see if she would visit with me over the phone. He told her my name, Elizabeth Jones, before handing over the phone to me.

"I am sorry we have to talk on the phone, but I am up to my ass gluing folders for my husband's company."

Not expecting the 'ass' comment, I relaxed and smiled. From the moment I heard her speak, I knew this was going to be different. She shared her teaching history, and I shared mine. Suddenly, we found ourselves saying, "Oh, my God! It's like we are twins!" We continued talking about our experiences, and we laughed a lot.

I literally forgot that I was interviewing for a position. Needless to say, I had never had such an entertaining interview. An hour and a half later, I looked over at Mr. John James, who was now playing solitaire on his computer. A custodian popped in to say the parking lot was going to be resurfaced in thirty minutes and that all cars needed to be moved.

"Thanks, Beni," said Principal James. *Okay, Beni the custodian*, I silently wrote on the wall of my brain.

I heard Jean say over the phone, "You better go unless you want to spend the night! Once they block the exit, there is no getting off the campus." Then, she added, "I have really enjoyed our conversation and I think we will work well together. Unless you have any reservations, I am going to tell my boss that he's an idiot if he doesn't hire you!"

From the moment I heard her describe him as an idiot, I knew that we would make a great team. I thanked her for her time and said goodbye.

I then thanked Mr. James for his time, and he ended with his remark, "I'll call after I check references." Two hours later, I received his call offering me the position. Little did I know that accepting this teaching position would change my life forever. Yes, sometimes, it is good to work for idiots.

TWO

You're Kidding, Right?

In-service is the week before the official start date for the new academic year. Typically, teachers have five days of meetings and only one day to work in and prepare their classrooms for the first day of school. In 1993, without the convenience of the internet, in-service agendas were mailed in advance to staff. I had received mine, along with the typical 'welcome back' introduction letter, the last week of July. I was ready to take on my new school.

At 7:45 a.m., I pulled into the parking lot of my new campus. North Gate High School was a small school in South Texas. It had excellent ratings based on student performance on the state-mandated tests. The high school had 400 students, and the middle school had 250 students. The small classes and high student scores had caught my attention. The entrance to the teacher's parking lot was under construction, and I was greeted with a line of traffic. As I was nervous about the first day, I thought that arriving early was paramount. Wanting to make the right impression on the first day, I had spent hours the night before choosing just the right outfit. The welcome letter had said casual dress, but since jeans wouldn't make the right statement, I chose a gray shirt dress and black sandals. Standing five feet, four inches tall with shoulder-length brown hair that I parted to the side and wore down, I wore red glasses (which gave me that serious yet professional look, I thought).

My husband's promotion couldn't have come at a worse time in my career. I had spent seven years building a Spanish program at Carson High School in North Texas, including organizing immersion trips to Spain. We then moved to East Texas, where I had doubled the student enrollment in the Spanish program and had begun an immersion program there, as well. In fact, I had recently returned from a two-week trip to Spain with fifteen eighth-graders, plus their parents. I was just getting back my momentum when my husband received the news that he would be moving to a bigger television market. Now, I was starting over again in a new school with new colleagues and new students.

Having only spoken to my department chair over the phone during my interview, and for over an hour, I remembered laughing with her more than anything. Today, I would finally get to place a face with a name. The first day of in-service always began with breakfast and new staff introductions. I would be introduced to a new faculty, and I had that awful, queasy feeling in the pit of my stomach. I couldn't help thinking about my old school and how comfortable I would have been joining them for breakfast. As I parked in the designated faculty lot, I was nervously rehearsing what to say after my introduction. My first words had to make a good impression on the faculty if I was going to be welcomed right away.

Suddenly, my mind flashed back to my first day at Webster ISD with Bobby J, his fishing pole, and Peepers the Rooster. I was a college student assigned to work as a teacher's aide in a very rural East Texas school district. Having driven forty-five minutes on a long and winding country road lined with corn fields, I remember pulling into a gravel parking lot and staring at an old, red building and thinking, *This can't be it. An entire school district is in one old building?* As I wobbled across the gravel in heels, a gentleman wearing starched, creased jeans and a long sleeve pearl-button shirt greeted me. He was carrying a fishing pole and tackle box. "Well, hello, young lady. You look a little lost."

"Yes, sir, can you tell me where the office is?"

"Right through those doors on the right. Have a great day, young lady."

I walked up to the main doors of the building only to be greeted by a rooster on the steps. *Uh-oh,* I thought, *what do I do now?*

At that moment, I heard the tires of a pick-up truck grinding against the gravel and a voice yelling, "Don't worry! He won't hurt you! Go right on in."

Okay. I am a city girl. I don't do roosters. Slowly, I stepped toward the door saying, "Hello, nice rooster." *What am I doing talking to a chicken? Where am I?* The rooster started flapping his wings and squawking as he strutted back and forth. Fortunately, a lady came to my rescue and moved the rooster out of the way: "Shoo, Peepers! Git now. May I hep you, hun?"

"Yes, ma'am. My name is Elizabeth Jones. I'm here as a teacher's aide for Mrs. Brown this semester."

"Okay, come on in! Sorry about the rooster. He belongs to one of the students. He's a pet and follows him to school every day. When he was a chick, the kids would play with him and feed him, so he thinks he belongs here. City girl are ya?"

"Yes, ma'am."

"Well, you just missed Bobby J, the principal, so I guess you can come visit with him tomorrow. Of course, if the fish aren't biting, you might just see him today. Have a seat. Mrs. Brown will be here in a minute."

That, I realized, *explains the gentleman with the fishing pole.* By the time that I had finished that first fall semester, Peepers and I had become great friends (only because I would bring him chicken feed in a baggy and would toss some feed on the ground away from the door). Wouldn't you know, that cocky old rooster learned my car and would come strutting towards me as soon as I pulled in looking for his treat!

Wow. I had come a long way. At least, I would not be negotiating with a rooster today, this first day at my new school. As I turned off the ignition and took a deep breath, something caught my attention. I looked up through the windshield in the direction of the school entrance only to see one woman running across the lawn toward another woman. I watched with curiosity. The woman running was wearing baggy khaki shorts, a navy T-shirt, and white tennis shoes. She had short, brown hair; slim, rectangular glasses; and skinny, freckled legs. As she ran after the other woman, she hollered, "Hey! Are you my new Spanish teacher?"

The other woman, startled, turned and said, "No, I'm the new English teacher. Can I help you?"

"No, not unless you are my new Spanish teacher. Are you sure you don't teach Spanish? You have brown hair and glasses."

Before the new English teacher could answer, the lively lady who had chased her was already entering the building. I could now put a face with the voice on the phone. *That has to be my department chair*, I thought, and *I am definitely overdressed.*

Finally emerging from my car, I walked into the building. Immediately, my nostrils were struck with a strong and unpleasant tar smell. My eyes were assaulted by bright, blue lockers and old, gray floor tiles. My footsteps echoingly pounded out their hollow notes on the main entry hall's floor.

The 'welcome back' letter had outlined the day's agenda.

Breakfast: 8:00-8:30 in the cafeteria.

Welcome Back Speech and Introduction of New Staff: 8:30-9:00.

Discussion of Curriculum Data and Ideas for Improvement: 9:00-11:30.

Lunch: 11:30-12:30.

Curriculum Discussion by Departments: 12:30-
end of work day.

The rest of the week was also devoted to curriculum
development. Obviously, North Gate was committed
to a five-year curriculum project that would consume
all of our teacher in-service days, plus an extra six days
that North Gate had petitioned from the state of Texas
to occur at other points within the school year. From
the look of the agenda, lunch was the only bright spot
of the day. *Sigh.*

Following the crowd down the hall and into the cafeteria, I could hear my department chair questioning the
new staff members. Tapping her on the shoulder, I said,
"Jean, my name is Elizabeth. I think you are looking for
me?"

"Thank goodness! I found you! I've been asking everybody! Did you see me going crazy?"

"Uh, yes, I did. You were hard to miss. I am curious
about your shorts, though. I think I am overdressed."

"Not at all. You see, I was a traveling teacher last year.
This year, I get a room—number 13. I hope it's not
an omen. I went to find all my things from last year,

and everything was dumped on the floor and stacked in a wheelbarrow in the middle school building—in a wheelbarrow, can you believe it? I am not about to haul all my stuff from building to building in heels, which accounts for why I've disregarded today's dress code that was spelled out to us in the 'welcome back' letter. This is my 'business casual attire' for the day!"

"Anyway, enough of that. First things first. Nobody but 'admin' calls me 'Jean.' Please, call me 'Mala.' It's my nickname."

"Ahhh, as in the 'bad one' en español, sí?"

"¡Claro que sí! (of course), I'm usually in trouble. What can I call you? Got a nickname?"

"Sure, how about 'Swan'? It's a name from my childhood."

"Swan—because you are graceful?"

"No, because I have a long neck."

"I like it. Come on, Swan, we have work to do."

Without so much as a cup of morning coffee, I followed Mala out of the cafeteria. She called out to the principal and announced that we couldn't make the breakfast. With authority in her voice, she informed him, " The two of us have to meet right away. We'll be in the old industrial tech room, if you need us!" Francine Davis, the assistant principal, reminded Mala as we exited past her that we needed to sign in and attend all the meetings.

"Got it, Francie. Don't worry, you can write me up if I forget."

"That's our assistant principal. She's new as of last year. She has two master's degrees and likes to control things. Not real sure about her yet. She's single and loves her work. You know the type right??"

"I don't even know her, yet."

"Ah, you're a diplomat. I like that. Anyway, rumor is— she's lonely, and all she has is school, so she's always in our business. What else does she have to do?"

With that, Mala led me down a hallway. "They're still mad at me for having a microwave in one of my class-rooms last year. It caught fire during spring semester, so I threw it out the window. You'd think they woul-da been happy that I didn't burn down the room—or worse, any of my students! But, nooo! Instead, I got the no-unauthorized-electronics speech and the liability-to-the-district speech."

"Oh, yes. I know that speech well," I commiserated. "Where are we going?"

"To the industrial tech room. Do you want the good news or the bad news first?"

"There's already bad news? Good grief! I haven't even been asked yet to introduce myself to the faculty. I'll take the good news first, please."

"The industrial tech room is going to be your room this year," Mala said as she unlocked a classroom door. As I stood on the threshold, she flipped on light switches. Nothing happened. An old, musty smell immediately insulted my nostrils. We continued standing in darkness and listening to a low, buzzing-drumming-humming electrical noise. Tubular fluorescent lights stubbornly, slowly, and sequentially finally flickered on to illuminate the disaster area that lay before me. My eyes were aghast.

The walls were constructed of gray concrete cinder blocks painted over with even more gray. *Prison gray,* I thought. The concrete floor was covered in dust and rusty nuts and bolts from old machinery that had been moved against two long, opposing walls. The ceiling was twenty feet high with exposed metal ductwork and several ceiling-mounted box fans. On the doorway wall, and to my left, were metal cages standing approximately twelve feet tall. They appeared to house all kinds of additional, dusty equipment. Cautiously side-stepping debris, I entered. I was at a loss for words.

"It's not too bad if you ignore the old equipment you have to work around—not ideal, but it beats traveling to four different buildings like I had to do last year. I'm not sure what you call these things any more, but Mr. James assured me that all this equipment would get moved out of your way."

"This is my room? Holy crap! Now, I'm afraid to even ask about the bad news."

"You have to share it with the drama teacher."

"You are kidding, right?" My gawking eyes swallowed the scene before me once again. "Mala, you have got to be pulling my leg. Two totally different classes of two totally different subjects having to share the same cavernous room—and look at all this crap in here! Talk about clutter. Look at this over here." I walked over to where some black plastic was not fully covering one of the machines. "These sharp metal edges and corners are going to hurt somebody." I slightly lifted the black plastic from another piece of equipment and peeked underneath it. "Oh, great. Blades? Blades and gears, wheels and pulleys, handles and cranks—Mala, my so-called classroom is filled with Medieval torture devices—what in the world? Where do these metal, double doors lead, Mala?" Grabbing the two long, metal handles, I pushed them open and found myself staring at the student parking lot. "Mala, what's going to stop a student who wants to skip class from skipping right on out these doors?"

"Don't worry about those. Beni just has the chains and padlock off right now. He'll put those back on before school starts." I'm thinking, *Chains and padlock?*

Speaking the next syllables as separate words, I said, "Are-you-kid-ding-me? Oh. Well, isn't this just dandy? My voice is echoing, coming back to me. Now, won't that be a fun concentration disrupter? And no wonder, Mala—this room is nothing but a cinderblock cavern with a twenty-foot ceiling. Oh, no; oh, no, Mala. How can two teachers possibly conduct their own classes in here without any kind of wall or partition to divide their space—uh, they are going to give me desks, right?—you know, the basic classroom set up?"

"Are you through?" I dropped my head, staring at the grimy concrete floor, hands on my hips. "Before you panic, just breathe. It's temporary, so don't worry about it. Just look at all the space you will have to work with. We'll get to all the details later—trust me! Oh, and this space over here, behind these two paneled walls, this is going to be the clinic."

My jaw dropped. "Are you kidding me?"

"To answer that question, nope, I'm not kiddin' ya—well, except for the desks, you'll get those—but otherwise, not joking. This is it, Kiddo. But—I have been thinking about ways to fix it up...you know, like hanging things from the ceiling, putting posters on the walls."

"Jean, I mean Mala, I don't think I can do this. Seriously."

"Okay, seriously, here's the deal. I know it's bad, but before you say anything else, think outside the box."

"Just how far out should I go?"

"Sarcasm, I like it!"

I couldn't take any more. Spinning around to head back toward the door, my toes kicked something. I looked down at the floor. A yellow helmet stared up at me. "Wait, this is a joke, right? You're trying to 'raz' the new teacher, right?"

"Hey, there's another helmet over here on this old work table." Mala picked it up and put it on her head. "Swan, put yours on, too."

I humored her. Now, we each had a helmet on our head. *What next?*

"These'll come in handy, don't ya think?" We each stood there staring at each other wearing yellow helmets on our head. "Now, let's go hide in my room for awhile."

Stunned, speechless, and wearing my hard hat, I followed Mala down the hall thinking, *What have I done?* Never in my ten years of teaching had I ever seen anything like this. I wanted to turn and run, but with the contract already signed, I was locked in for the year. At this late date, finding another position would be next to impossible.

I do have to admit, Mala's infectious personality did keep me expectantly curious for her next idea and the ones to surely follow. I found myself absorbed in her conversation. While we race-walked down one hallway and then another, she would wave her hands, point, and address everyone in her path. Her bubbly personality during my phone interview with her, I recalled, was what had captured my attention. Today, her enthusiasm—and her vision for that old, dilapidated, industrial classroom that was to be mine for the year—made me want to trust her instincts.

Always talking, she jumped from one new subject to another. Passing classrooms, she would make a sarcastic remark to her colleague friends, such as, "Hey! You aren't skippin' breakfast, are ya? Francine asked me to take names today."

The replies were just as sarcastic. "Yeah, right. Remember, you broke fire code. You, Jean, will never be her assistant."

"That was my plan all along." She laughed and whipped into Room 13. "Here it is, lucky number 13. This is my new room. I 'floated' in this room last year for Sixth-Grade Exploratory Language. I am hoping that, for this year, the number proves to be good luck.

"Inside all these plastic containers are bulletin board materials, borders, and posters. Ignore that pile of desks. All you and I need just to do our work for now are these two desks," she declared, as she dragged them into a clearing on the concrete floor. "Don't worry, we'll fix up that room of yours."

"I also want to apologize for not coming to the school during your interview. My husband was transferred here three years ago. He's in manufacturing and works as a plant manager. Now that manufacturing is going overseas, he lost his job. So, what does my Bob do? Why, he starts his own company, of course! In fact, the day of your interview, I was gluing three hundred navy blue folders for one of his clients. They ordered three thousand. Thank goodness, I didn't have to glue that many!"

"Oh, yeah, sorry about the tar smell." Mala apologized

in response to my sniffing nose and scrunched up face reacting to the acrid smell of burning rubber.

"What is that anyway?"

"They're fixin' the roof on our wing. We had such bad leaks last year that when it rained, my students had to wear trash bags on their heads to avoid the drips. Have a seat. Do you have any questions?"

"Are we going to smell tar all day?"

"Well, yes, I am afraid so. We have bets to see how many teachers get sick. Want in the pool?"

"Nooooo, just wondering why not do this in June when school is out? Makes too much sense?"

"Swan, you know if it makes sense, they don't do it. Now, nitty-gritty questions?"

"Yes, a million, but for starters—do you have my schedule of classes? Wait a minute; back the train up. You're not kidding about students wearing trash bags, are you?"

"Nope, not kidding at all. Lucky for me the kids thought that wearing trash bags was more fun than learning Spanish. We pretended to be stranded in the rain forest. Let's see... schedules—yep, got 'em right here. I bet Mr. James didn't tell you what you would be teaching, did he?"

"He said you and I would work that out."

"Oh, I bet he did," Mala said in a smarmy, sarcastic tone, "because he hasn't finished the master schedule yet, and school starts in a week. Great, just great. I get to do his job, too."

Clearly irritated, she explained Principal James' background. "John James attended and graduated from North Gate High School. He was the star quarterback his senior year. The district hired him. He taught Health Science and coached varsity football but then was promoted to the principalship of the middle school while still retaining only the high school coaching position. He must excel at coaching because North Gate won district last year. However, don't expect him to support us, his high school faculty this year. He was successful as the middle school principal for three years. Now, as the high school principal, he is overwhelmed because he's still coaching football."

"That explains my phone call to apply for this position. He introduced himself as the middle school principal, but then stumbled and said that he meant high school principal."

Mala looked at her watch. "Come on, let's meet the faculty. Oh, wait! Put on your hard hat, and follow my lead."

"Huh? Wait, what? We're gonna wear these helmets into the cafeteria? For in-service? In front of the principal? For me to meet the faculty? For them to see me for the first time? Why?"

"Bullshit protectors."

THREE

When's Lunch?

We raced into the cafeteria wearing our hard hats as Mr. James was welcoming the faculty. Mala announced to the assembled staff, "Just showed her where she'll be teaching. She was speechless."

The faculty laughed. Mr. James, glancing at his watch, responded, "Well, so glad you both could join us. Do I want to know about your new hat?"

"Oh, these?" Mala tap-tapped the top of hers. "Why, I found these fine millinery specimens in the classroom you assigned her, Mr. James. They're bullshit protectors. No matter what you tell us today, we're prepared." Again, the faculty laughed (maybe a little more nervously this time).

"Hmmm, I see." He continued, "Now then, I would like

each department to introduce their new people, and we will start with the Foreign Language Department. Mrs. Smith, since you are already out of your seat, will you introduce your new teacher?"

"You bet, Boss! This is Elizabeth Jones. She is a native Texan and has ten years of teaching experience. I figured if Mr. James didn't scare her off during the interview, then she would be great for the department. We're not sure of our schedules yet, but trust me, she will be teaching Spanish. Now, we just need to brainstorm how to set up that old industrial room she'll be using and hope that she doesn't change her mind." As the faculty chuckled in knowing agreement, Mala handed the microphone to me as if to say, 'take a bow.'

"I would like to say how excited I am to be a part of your faculty. Yes, I am a little speechless about my room, but I think this team of Smith and Jones will be a great one! I know that I probably picked the worst week to call and inquire about teaching positions, so I do want to thank you, Mr. James, for taking a chance and hiring me. Also, I look forward to meeting you all."

Handing the microphone back to Mr. James, I took a seat next to where Mala had gone to sit. As soon as I felt the chair on my back, I sensed instant relief as

Mr. James proceeded with the remainder of the new-faculty introductions.

Like a schoolgirl, Mala covertly slid a folded-up note in front of me. As her new partner in crime, I quietly opened its folds while keeping my eye contact directly on the principal. As soon as he focused away from my direction, I read Mala's words: *'Good job diplomat. Way to brown-nose. You'll do just fine.'*

Mr. James finished summarizing some of the curriculum changes that would take place, and then he introduced Francine Davis, the assistant principal. Francine's light blue suit complemented her blonde hair and blue eyes. She stood five feet ten; slender; and wore her hair back away from her face and tied up in a tight bun. This gave her a professional appearance. Francine gave her welcoming speech, adding that this was going to be a challenging year because of the fact that we would be rewriting our curriculum. With that, she dimmed the lights and began her power point presentation of the curriculum project timeline. As soon as it advanced to the third slide, however, the computer froze. Francine excused herself and began to reboot the system. One of the teachers called out, "Oh great! Now, we'll be late to lunch." Everyone groaned, or maybe laughed, or maybe groaned. Mr. James interrupted that with a 'settle down and let's get back on track' harrumph.

Mala now passing notes with another faculty member caught my eye. I could see that their notes, slid sneakily down the cafeteria table to each other, were a series of drawings depicting the administration versus the teachers. One such note read, "Notice that the tar smell seems to get worse when Francine begins to speak! This has GOT to be foreshadowing." Mala released a sudden, explosive cackle!

Francine's lips puckered sternly. "Jean, do you have a joke that you want to share while we wait?"

"No, Francine. I am so sorry for being rude, but I was telling Jeb how much I love the background colors of your presentation. Please continue."

Francine, not responding to the sarcasm nor to the obvious non-explanation for that loud cackle, looked irritated. However, she continued once she noticed her computer was back online.

Surveying the cafeteria, I noticed that none of the faculty was really paying attention—including Mr. James, leaning back against the cafeteria wall with his chair balanced on its two back legs. What's more, I couldn't help but notice how most everyone was covering his or her noses (with hands, with napkins, or even with one of Francine's curriculum-change handout packets) because the smell from the tar was growing noticeably more fetid. Not helping the audio presentation one bit, the motor to the generator located right outside the cafeteria windows was gratingly annoying. We were all frustrated and distracted. For some degree of distracting relief, Mala continued sketching the admins while also drafting haikus about Francine's presentation. I continued occupying myself by studying those around me.

For example, there was Jeb (biology), sitting on the other side of Mala, wearing bleach-splotched jeans and a Texas Longhorn T-shirt. Over time, I came to learn that Jeb was a practical joker and a risk taker. He was always devising new experiments for his students, most of which were practical and standard experiments for a biology class. However, he would sometimes set up riskier experiments, such as having the students place their faces in ice cold water and then measuring their heart rates. Go figure, when the superintendent just happened to walk by his lab and see students gasping for air, he was called to her office. Jeb was that mad scientist who brewed coffee in the lab next to his biology specimens. Who knows what we were really drinking!

On the other side of me sat Alice the drama teacher, reading scripts. Alice showed off her physique wearing a royal blue, Thespian polo shirt and a blue jean miniskirt. Her clothing was clearly rebelling against what surely was her more than forty years of age. Eventually, I discovered more from my observations of and inter-actions with Alice. When her husband had lost his job, she had gone back to the classroom after having been a teacher some years earlier. Alice moved through space with a dramatic flair and an energy (along with her dyed, jet-black mane) that stirred the air. Her ex-pressive talk was as much with her hands—and indeed, with her entire body—as with her mouth.

Next to Alice was a young man named Dexter, Dex for short, who sported a pale blush, cotton polo shirt, khaki pants, and a pale blue-and-teal striped tie. This look was topped off by his bed-head, mousey-brown mop. I could guess, because of the language arts book he was perusing, that he was an English teacher. He and Alice seemed to be close. I slid a note over to Mala asking if those two to my left were good—as in, re-ally good—friends. Mala's note back to me, on which she had drawn a winking smiley face, answered in two words: "who knows?" She later explained that Dex had been hired just the year before, and Alice had been as-signed as his teacher mentor. He, in turn, helped her with technical aspects of her lighting, sound, and set construction for her productions.

In the back of the cafeteria was a table of coaches dressed in their typical garb of athletic shorts and

T-shirts. Coaches usually tolerated in-service, as it fell right in the middle of their boot camp and their attention was clearly focused on the new season and not curriculum. If they were not reading magazines out of sheer boredom, then they were going over plays for their upcoming football season.

Finally, Francine ended her presentation by announcing which rooms would be devoted to departmental curriculum meetings. Mala jumped up and tapped me on the shoulder saying, "Let's go! Room 13!"

"But that wasn't one of the—"

Francine stopped us both with her voice. "Jean, where will Foreign Language meet today?"

"Why, we shall be in my new room, Room 13, where else?" answered Mala oh-so-sweetly but sarcastically.

Room 13— it was a menagerie of boxes, plastic containers, shelves filled with books and folders, student desks, and chairs that had all been piled up in the middle of the room from summer maintenance work. Two of the walls had chalk boards; one wall was all windows; and the remaining wall was gray-painted cinder blocks. CDs, which through some technique had been shaped into the design of fish, hung suspended from the ceiling and cast their reflected rays of sunlight, like fish bejeweled with diamond sparkles, on the bare chalk boards.

"You would think that they could at least try to arrange the desks instead of making one big pile," Mala sighed.

"I like the fish."

"Sixth-Grade Exploratory Spanish. It was an under-the-sea unit."

"What an awesome idea!"

"According to Mr. James, they're a fire hazard, and he wants them taken down. I promised him that I could handle a little classroom fire with the trusty-dusty fire extinguisher, should such a 'CD sparkly fish-fire' ever occur. I also promised I would take them down...just didn't say when."

Mala got down to business as we sat in two chairs that we pulled from the top of the chair mound. "As far as our schedules go, together we have three sections of Spanish I; three sections of Spanish II; two sections of Spanish III; one section of Spanish IV; one ESL; and one eighth-grade class. I will take the ESL, the eighth grade, one of the Spanish II, two of the Spanish III, and one Spanish IV. That gives you three Spanish I, two Spanish two, and one study hall. We will both sponsor the National Spanish Honor Society. Whatcha think, Swan?"

I glanced with skepticism into my future for this next school year—the schedule of three preps in the old industrial tech room shared with drama classes on one side and the school nurse on the other. *What did I think?* I didn't know what to think. In a flash of hopeful imagination, I wished *Candid Camera* would surprise me at any moment, and an unseen voice would tell me to smile because I was on candid camera—their trade-mark line of that old TV show. I'm not sure what I was thinking because I was still digesting my room situation. "Mala, I think it's going to be one crazy year, that's what I think."

"More than you know." As soon as Mala finished that last word, a loud fire alarm blared.

"Oh, no! Is this for real?" I asked, hearing the alarm in my own voice.

"Probably. This building is so old. C'mon, let's go. Oh, first—do you see any of my CD sparkly fish on fire?"

I assured her no.

Laughing as we exited Room 13, we were joined by Jack the physics teacher.

"Here we go again, electrical problems," Jack said under his breath.

"Jack, this is Elizabeth, who—" Mala began but then stopped to ask, "Did you see Jeb?

"No, not lately. You know Jeb. He's always hiding in his lab. Probably working on a new Frankenstein prototype."

"Yeah, but he'll be 'written up' if he doesn't exit the building. Take Elizabeth, and I'll go get his ass!"

Jack motioned with his hand for me to follow.

"Is it always like this?" My inquiring mind wanted to know.

"Like what—crazy, unbelievable mayhem? Don't tell me you came from a 'normal' school where things ran smoothly? What's that like?"

"Well, yes, I guess. It was nice, organized, and I have to say much more modern and new. I know it's the quality of the staff and not the building that makes a good education—but really, tar smell and a fire drill on day one! Throw me a bone, will ya! Just how old is this building, anyway?"

"Thirty years and still counting. Notice the perfect timing—as in, they fix the roof giving us this terrific tar smell right before and as school starts? Just wait until the kids have to smell this all day. Okay," Jack directed me, "out this door and over by the track."

Jack was older with graying temples, I noticed. In time, I discovered that Jack was divorced and still held bitterness about his wife who had left him when he had lost his corporate job. He, also, was bitter about having to rely on teaching for an income.

"This is where we sit until the bell rings to reenter the building—and look, here comes the mad scientist with Mala. Yep, he's all decked out in his uniform." The uniform, I observed, was Jeb's lab coat and protective glasses that dangled around his neck.

Mala was scolding Jeb for not leaving the building at the sound of the alarm. Walking behind them was Alice the drama teacher holding her head. Mala, Jack, Jeb, Alice, and I all sat together on a wooden bleacher, engaging in idle chat while we waited for the re-entry bells to ring. Dex, I was informed, had to exit on the other side of the building.

"Don't you just love the 102-degree mornings in the summer?" asked Jack. He must have noticed how I kept looking at my watch, surmising that I believed my cheap but practical watch held the answer to how much longer we might have to sit and wait. Ten minutes passed, but those exit bells were still clanging. Now, I wished that I had worn shorts. Sweat was running down my back and my head was pounding.

I noticed Alice holding her head, swaying, and squinting down at the dirt and bits of dried, yellowed grass. "Are you okay, Alice?"

Mala, too, noticed. "What's wrong, Alice? You look very pale."

"Mala, I think I'm—" and down she went. Jeb immediately bent to fan Alice with the hem of his stained lab coat.

Mala hollered to Mr. James, "Boss! Get the nurse! We're losing one!" Mr. James quickly made a call on his walkie-talkie. Within seconds, Francine and Mary the nurse, along with Principal James, bound up the bleacher steps.

"What's wrong?" asked Mary.

"I think it was the presentation that did it," Jeb flatly stated.

"Jeb, this is no time for jokes," scolded Mr. James. I noticed that Francine appeared to take great umbrage at Jeb's remark.

"Did she hit her head?" asked Mary.

"No, she was already starting to sit down before she ever hit the dirt," replied Mala.

"Let's get her to the clinic." Francine ordered Jeb and Jack to carry Alice to Mary's make-shift clinic (a.k.a., my 'industrial tech-turned-Spanish-shared-with-drama-and-the-nurse classroom') while she herself escorted the faculty back into the building despite the still-ringing bells.

"We have a clinic now?" asked Jack.

"Temporarily," answered Nurse Mary. "I'm using the old photography lab in the corner of what used to be the industrial tech room. Elizabeth and I are going to be very close neighbors."

Jeb and Jack dutifully carried Alice to the clinic's little corner with Mary following closely behind them. They placed their charge on the clinic bed. Mala and I, drenched in our own sweat, trudged back to Room 13 to finish our planning for the year.

Suddenly, Mr. James' voice boomed over the loud speaker. "Teachers, due to the tar smell and the fire alarms ringing and one of our teachers fainting, go ahead and take lunch now. It's 11:00 a.m., so meet back in your rooms by 12:30 p.m. By then, we should have things fixed. Again, take lunch now, and report back at 12:30 p.m."

Finally. Lunch.

FOUR

Drunken Noodles
& Papel Picado

"Let's go to lunch! Head 'em up, move 'em out!" exclaimed Jeb. "Whose turn is it to drive?"

"Not mine," said Jack.

"Not mine," said Mala.

"Don't look at me," said I. "I don't have a clue where I am."

"Okay, then," said Jeb, "my car is over here. Follow me. Is everyone okay with Thai food? Linzey Faith came by before the fire alarm and said we should meet at Thai Buffet for lunch."

"Ahhhh, not Linzey Faith," whined Jack. "All she'll do is correct us. You know she will."

"Jack, behave. You know Linz doesn't have many friends. "You can tolerate forty-five minutes with her," Mala admonished. Besides, you just might learn something. She's certainly my candidate for *Jeopardy* because she knows everything."

"As she will tell ya, too," reacted Jack.

Mala, in the coming days, described Linzey Faith Reinerd to me as a stern and meticulous librarian—as in a 'look-at-the-books-but-don't-touch' stern and meticulous librarian. She was not married and had no children—not even the furry kind. That is why, Mala postulated, Linzy Faith is hoveringly protective of her books. Mala told me that even in casual chitchat conversations, Linzey Faith tends to be quite precise and fussy about diction, meaning about word choices. Mala said that Linzey Faith does a whole lot of 'correcting.' *Oh, dear,* I thought, *a grammar perfectionist.* Of course, I could see Mala's point about that making people uncomfortable to be around her. Perhaps Mala best captured the essence of Linzey Faith, though, by saying that while, yes, she is 'different' and saw things through her own unique lens, she nevertheless would do anything to help anyone from among the faculty group. While on the one hand, I was all prepared, in advance, to cringe around Linzey Faith Reinerd the librarian (a bit of a prissy sounding name, I must add), on the other hand, I had a soft spot in my heart for her. By the way, as was explained to me, she insisted on being called 'Linzey Faith' by those in her friendship circle and "Ms. Reinerd" by other faculty, staff, students, and parents. If anyone called her only Linzey, or just Faith—well, that person did not really know her.

Changing the subject, Mala asked me, "How ya doin' so far?"

With a little bit of a laugh, I responded, "I feel better now that I'm away from the tar smell. Thanks."

"Here we are," Jeb announced, "and oh, look—there's Linzey Faith, waving us in to the parking space she's picked out for us. How much do y'all want to bet that she's probably already been inside and requested a table in a far corner away from the smokers?" snarked Jeb as he parked the car (as per Linzey Faith's air-traffic controller type hand signals).

Inside, the restaurant was small and crowded. Sure enough, the hostess led us to a corner table for five that, yes, Linzey Faith had already arranged to save for us. Actually, Linzey Faith led the hostess who led us. I noted that Linzey Faith was of medium height with long brown hair and green eyes. With her cargo pants, mostly purple tie-dyed T-shirt, brown and turquoise dream-catcher earrings, and backpack slung over one shoulder, Ms. Linzey Faith Reinerd reminded me of a throw-back to the sixties à la trekker-across-Europe flower child.

"Linzey Faith, this is Elizabeth, my new Spanish teacher." Mala motioned to the group to sit down. "We've broken her in just right. First, she will be teaching in what had been the industrial tech room, sharing it with Alice and her drama classes. Next, she has a headache from the tar; and, oh, let's see, she helped carry Alice to the clinic. All in all, she's had a 'Tom Terrific' day."

"I had heard several teachers went home sick from the tar smell. So, Alice fainted, huh? How is she now?" asked Linzey Faith.

"Who knows? I think that Dex probably followed her home," replied Jeb.

"By the way," said Linzey Faith, "did anyone mention to you all that it was the roof repairs that caused the fire drill?" For good measure, for maximum impact, she added, "Oh! And did you all know that we will be starting school next week without air conditioning?" A proud and smug little smile grew on Linzey Faith's face.

"What, no air?!" Jack angrily barked. "They failed to

mention that in the 'welcome-back-how-was-your-summer' speech!"

"What?! How did you hear this? I hope that's just a rumor!" wailed Mala.

"You have got to be kidding, Linzey Faith! No way," flatly stated Jeb, "the students will survive that!"

(I noticed that Linzy Faith grew this smug, quite proud-of-herself, little smirk of a smile. *Mission accomplished*, I thought. She managed to deliver some news that had found its mark after all!)

With a groan of exasperation at the horrid thought of no air conditioning for the entire first week of school—in South Texas, where the temperature mark could easily hit 110 in the shade—Jeb motioned to the waitress that we were ready to order.

Our waitress made her rounds to each one of us, myself being last. "I think I need those Drunken Noodles, please!"

Just for good measure, Linzey Faith inserted one more gem of hers: "I eavesdropped on Mr. James talking with the engineers outside the library just as I was leaving for lunch. It's no rumor, Jean. The engineers are the ones who told the principal, 'Sorry. No AC next week.'" Linzey Faith's grin grew, I observed, as Mala's countenance fell in defeat.

By now, I was really questioning my decision to teach at North Gate High School. The small campus and the even smaller class sizes were no longer appealing to me. No air conditioning for the first few days of school; the raucous sounds of roof repairs for who knew how long; the putrid stench of tar for an equally unknown amount of time; trying to teach in that old, dusty-musty industrial tech room for the entire year—*ugh. No way will I survive day one. Why would I even want to—*

Mala interrupted my destructively negative thoughts with a warning in my right ear: "Psst, Linzey Faith is our informant. Watch what you tell her and say around her." *No kidding.*

Meanwhile, as we ate our food (Linzey Faith prissily attempting chopsticks), Jack decided to call the office and check on the condition of the building. Doing some quick, hard pondering in order to resolve the dilemma that by now had taken up residence in my mind, and in order to make a deliberative decision as to whether I should continue riding with this motley crew or jump off my horse and high-tail it out of there, I studied each one, going clockwise around the table and starting to my left: Jeb, Linzey Faith, Jack, and Jean (a.k.a., Mala-by-my-side). I realized that these people were the only reason I would ever survive what for me was a new and transitional year in my career—and indeed, in my life. I hoped, I hoped, that we could share lunch on a regular basis because being with this motley crew was like a night at the comedy club. They were the balm for my sad and scared-sick soul. *Why am I hearing more pounding? Oh, that's inside my head. My head is pounding.* Mala must have glanced over at me and noticed that I was massaging my temples in circular motions with my fingertips. She rubbed my right shoulder to comfort and reassure me. In turn, I gave her a slight, sideways smile, intended to be visible through the crook of my arm. I think she saw it because she nodded and gave me a consoling wink of understanding and camaraderie.

I sat up straight; inhaled through my nose and exhaled out my mouth to the count of three; repeated twice more; and then proceeded to eat my Drunken Noodles. With a fork.

"Good news! Mr. James has dismissed the faculty for the day. We are to meet tomorrow at 7:30 a.m., instead of 8:30, to make up for lost time. I just got off the phone with Kathleen, the secretary."

"Really? We can go?" *Should I be skeptical,* I admonished myself, *after so soon finding my confidence to forge ahead with these new colleagues of mine?*

"Let's take advantage of an afternoon off!" encouraged Jeb. "I'm going back to lock up my lab, and then go to the lake, rent a boat, and cruise the waves!

"Oh, great! Yep, that's our cue. We've got the 'green light' to go where we please and do what we want!" Mala picked up the check and began adding everyone's share of the bill.

"Thanks, you guys. See you all tomorrow—and please, tell me it's not like this every day?"

"Ah, naaagh. It gets worse—but you will, for sure, come back tomorrow, right?" asked Jack.

"Don't say that, you idiot!" Mala punched him in the arm. "I need a Spanish teacher, and where would I find another one at this late juncture, huh?"

Jeb marked his goodbye with a sailor's salute, but then with the same hand and pointed index finger, he made the stereotypical 'circling crazy gesture' while pointing to both Jack and Mala. He made me chuckle. *Am I really gonna be working with these three stooges, plus the 'rule-and-reign-control-the-train librarian, Linzey Faith? Why, yes. Yes, I am. This is going to be interesting.* As we drove away from Thai Buffet, I honestly couldn't wait for tomorrow.

For the rest of the week, (having wised up), I wore shorts and tennis shoes. Mala and I would squeeze in two hours each day in Room 13 (following each day's full-faculty meetings in which we were regaled with the delights of such information as Handling Bloodborne Pathogens; Performing CPR; and Recognizing and Reporting Child Abuse). We dutifully aligned our lesson plans with the new curriculum directives.

Jeb, Jack, and Linzey Faith stopped by each day to eat lunch with us in Mala's room. For interesting conversational fodder, Linzey Faith would bring the library's latest magazines, which would then prompt lively discussions on the stories that grabbed our attention the most. *National Geographic* articles were the most fun. I recall that on one day of in-service, she was excited that she was bringing an article—*Isolated Nomads Under Siege in the Amazon Jungle*—about indigenous cultures that she figured Mala and I could use for our culture units.

"Oh, yeah—hey! This would be great for our museum unit! We could use the Museo de Antropología in Mexico City as our model. What do you think, Swan?"

"Swan?!" queried Jack and Jeb and Linzy Faith, in unison (reminding me of a Greek chorus, as I stabbed my next bite of black olives-spinach-and feta cheese salad).

"Oh, that's her nickname," said Mala.

"For 'graceful?'" asked Linzy Faith.

"No, for my long neck," I answered, solving their mystery. "As for this article, I love the idea! We could assign student groups each an indigenous tribe to research, and each group could ultimately design an exhibit of their tribe as the culminating event of the unit. Linzey Faith, this is brilliant! Thanks so much!" Linzey Faith beamed with satisfaction that she had done something to please us, I sensed.

Jack and Jeb both, leaning over Mala's pimento cheese sandwich on whole wheat, ogled upside down upon the magazine photos of those half-naked clad females who were pictured among the *Isolated Nomads Under Siege in the Amazon Jungle.*

Mala rolled her eyes. "Jack and Jeb! What are we here—in seventh grade? Boys, what have I had to tell you in past years when coming into my room to hang out for our lunches?"

With a hang-dog look, Jack replied, "Unsnap 'em and hang 'em on a hook on the wall." Mala licked an index finger, snagged a corner of the page, and with her own snap movement—flipped to the next. *Oh, good, all expository information, thank goodness.*

Once, during this in-service week of lunch time fraternization, Jeb detailed to us the next science experiments that he was designing for his students. Jack warned him that some of those ideas were too 'cockamamy-risky' for the classroom. If Jack wasn't convincing, Linzey Faith (who knew everything) would interject her opinion, welcomed or not. For example, he told our lunch-bunch that he had just ordered a red lionfish for his biology room aquarium.

"A red lionfish from South Africa?" Linzey Faith furrowed her brows and tilted her head questioningly.

"The one and only," smirked Jeb.

Linzey Faith continued. "You do know they are poisonous, right, Jeb? Why, the red lionfish is quite the invasive, venomous coral reef fish. Natively, they are found in the warm waters of the Indo-Pacific region, but lately, they've become such a problem in the Caribbean Sea, even expanding their range along the East Coast of the United States. Because they are a relatively new fish species, though, other predator fish can't figure out how to eat those buggers. The lionfish, you see, have such a cantankerous demeanor—kinda like you, Jack (I heard Jack grunt, maybe combined with a groan, a sort of a grunt-groan). I'm sure you know, Jeb, but still, a sting from a lionfish is extremely painful to humans and can cause nausea and breathing difficulties, albeit only rarely fatal. But surely, Jeb, you wouldn't dare take a chance on having one in your classroom aquarium, now would you? Anyhow, did you know, Jeb, that the lionfish eggs hatch in just two days, and—"

"I think we've got the picture, Linzey Faith," interrupted Mala, to all our relief.

"Whew. Who needs *Encyclopedia Britannica* when ya have Linzey Faith." I did not hear a question in Jack's voice but more of a flat, declarative statement.

"Of course, I know all that, Linzy Faith (Jeb stated rather defensively, in my view)—but does Mr. James? That's my whole point." Uttering this next in feigned innocence, "I just want to make his day a little more, um, interesting and challenging. Ha! Can't you just picture him now, having to pull his *Encyclopedia Britannica* from a bookshelf to look it up? That's what makes ordering lab supplies so much more fun for me!"

"Now, Jebster," retorted Jack, "it's fun until our principal fires your butt." Mala rolled her eyes, again. I shook my head in disbelief. Jeb truly was their mad scientist, if not rabble-rouser.

During this week of in-service meetings and planning time, Mala was a trooper. She stayed after school each late afternoon with me as we tried to give a thorough cleaning to a Spanish classroom-of-sorts, the space of which was almost usurped by old, industrial arts equipment. Following two afternoons of sweeping and coughing, we finally got smart and wore bandanas over our faces, looking like a couple of cattle rustlers—only cattle rustlers who donned yellow hard hats.

Finally, Friday had arrived. For once this week, only one meeting was scheduled, and that at 2:00 p.m. to discuss opening-day procedures. That meant that from morning until then, Mala and I were free to try and transform a space that looked more like a manufacturing plant into a colorfully festive, inviting, and efficiently-organized Spanish classroom—not forgetting that I would be sharing this fine setting with Theater Arts and the nurse's station! *How in the world are we gonna achieve this feat?*

The answer: I had the best help. Not only my department head/new friend, Mala, but also the nicest custodian in the world, Beni, short for Benjamín. Probably all teachers would vouch for the fact that making good friends with the school custodians (especially right off the bat when starting at a new campus) behooves them. Beni scrounged, found, and brought desks down for me to arrange in some workable configuration for my students. The old, two-door metal cabinet Beni had found from somewhere (who am I to inquire from where?)

was a blessing, too. It did not lock, but I could at least store some supplies, underneath which I could hide my purse, temporarily, for now. Mostly, I enjoyed speaking Spanish with Beni; he, in turn, shared some of his personal story. In order to save his family's lives, he had to leave Mexico. There, he had been an attorney for the government; however, when any new president takes office, the old regime leaves—one way or another. Thus, he and his family, in fear for their lives due to political persecution, had to flee to the United States. Beni started life over as a custodian. *Just when I'm feeling sorry for myself, I hear Beni's story? Okay, God, I 'get' it.*

Alice, also working in 'our' room, had the brilliant idea to use her drama group's flats as dividers so as to delineate our two distinct classroom areas. I approved of that idea, seeing that those would work. Mala and I followed Alice's direction in helping her carry, the gray-spatter painted and hinged flats to the right spots on the floor. We unfolded, and set up the three-fold muslin flats used typically as 'walls' for stage sets, to divide this warehouse into two distinct classrooms. As a result, my 'classroom' now had walls comprised of one metal cabinet and five gray theatre flats. *Why not? I'll play along for now, but this is gonna just be temporary, right?* I asked myself that, but any certain and sure answer was not forthcoming.

"Oh! It's 1:58 p.m.!" emoted Alice. " We've got our 2:00 p.m. meeting! C'mon, you two! We're gonna have to run. Can y'all run?"

"Yes, Alice, we can run," grunted Mala. "The question is whether we're too tired to run." I nodded in agreement as we flew down the hallway. We ran to the cafeteria, stopping only as we reached the double doors, at which time the three of us made a highly dignified entrance. Breathing heavily and covered in grime and dust, we made a fine appearance, I'm sure. *Oops. Mala and I forgot to wear our hard hats,* I lamented. With that thought, I smiled to myself, realizing that I was bonding and fitting in quite nicely here at my new school.

The faculty in-service meeting, the last one of this long week, ended at 3:00 p.m. Mala left me to go work in her own room: desk arrangement; teacher desk positioning; bulletin board decorations; and so many other unheralded tasks that all teachers do prior to the first day of school. At 4:30 p.m., Mr. James announced that the parking lot needed to be cleared of all vehicles. Shortly after his announcement, Beni stopped by to remind me of the construction.

"I remember learning about the nightly construction hours when I interviewed."

"Muy bien. Hasta mañana, Señora Jones."

"Si, Señor Beni. Hasta mañana. Oh! Hey, Beni! Is there a ladder, a really tall ladder, that I might use?"

"Sí, yes, I can find one for you, Miss. You better go on to your car. I will get ladder and lean it right here inside your door before I leave."

"Oh, gracias, Beni! I'm wanting to hang papel picado to give this warehouse some color."

"Ah, muy bien, Señora. I like that!"

Made from brightly-colored tissue paper, papel picado has intricate designs cut out of the paper that depict cultural scenes—such as the Aztec calendar, skulls and skeletons, folklórico dancers, Mariachi musicians, birds, suns, and fountains

"Hey, I like that idea!" Mala had entered just as I said that last to Beni, who departed to go find the ladder for me. "Swan, I'm gonna bring you some travel posters; I've already put enough up in my room, so I've got extras. Will bring you a glue gun, too—glue's already hot. Speaking of glue, don't wantcha to think that I'm bailing on you—but I am. I have got to go glue more folders for Bob's new business. Are you going to be okay?"

"Yes. I know that I'm gonna have to put in long hours this weekend to finish getting ready, but that's par for the course, right? I'm used to working weekends, and my husband is a trooper. Besides, Mike likes a challenge, and I think I've found a good one for him! See you Monday, Mala. Happy gluing—oh, well, not too happy, with glue and all. Raise your windows!" Mala chuckled, understanding my joke.

I gathered my purse and other personal items and walked to my car thinking, *What in the hell have I gotten myself into?* Entering my house that Friday evening, I saw that Mike was already home and busy going over the kids' weekend schedules.

"Hey, Sweetheart. How did today go? Any new surprises?"

"No, well, other than I may not have air conditioning Monday. I need to carve out some time to finish setting up my so-called room into a classroom. The custodian, Beni—who's wonderful, by the way—was going to find and leave me a ladder because I want to try and hang picado from the ceiling. Can you help me with that, I hope? Also, somehow, I need to glue posters on those drab, gray, cinder block walls. Oh, and I need an easel and some flip charts until I get a chalk board or dry erase board mounted on a wall. Let's see, I'm gonna also need—"

Mike cut me off with a knowing smile. "Looks like we're going shopping, Swan, and then yes, I'll go to North Gate with you."

"Thanks, I was hoping you would say that." After giving him a kiss of my gratitude on his cheek, I told him that I was heading to the nearest school supply store to buy those items I needed.

We rose early the next morning, did our wake-up routines as swiftly as possible, dropped our kids off at their early Saturday morning practices and activities, and then Mike and I headed to my North Gate campus, arriving by 8:30 a.m. Mr. James had arranged for the gate and the building to be open until noon, but only until noon, so as to allow teachers to have access to their classrooms for any last-minute, first-day-of-school preparations for Monday.

Mike and I unloaded boxes, not only those items of mine I had packed from my former school, but also all the new items that I had to purchase at the store the night before (with my own money, of course—certainly not from any budget given to us by the school, oh no). We carried the cumbersome boxes and plastic tubs from our SUV to just outside the door of the industrial tech room, setting each down until we had fully unloaded our vehicle. I unlocked the heavy steel door and flipped on the lights, explaining to Mike that we would have to wait, and wait, then wait some more for each tubular, fluorescent light—sequentially—to take its own, good, sweet time in turning on. These fluorescent lights were old, made obvious by the dust coating and the occasional dead insect once living but now fried and entombed inside the ridged plastic casing which overlay the tubular bulbs. As each temperamental fluorescent began to illuminate more and more of the space, Mike's eyes began a sweeping survey. "You weren't exaggerating at all! This is where they want you to teach?"

"Yes, and don't forget Alice the drama teacher and I get to share this space—oh, and with Nurse Mary and sick kiddos, as well."

"After standing in contemplative silence for a few long seconds (but faster than the fluorescents), he said, "Okey-doke. Let's see what we can do."

We slaved all morning. First, we climbed up and down the sixteen-foot ladder with its four-foot extension to hang papel picado. I would start at the top of the cinder block wall and tie the end to a pipe. Mike would carefully roll the ladder, with me precariously perched on top of it, and every five sections, I would tape the string (one-two-three-four-five, tape; one-two-three-four-five, tape) in between the squares, taping to another pipe, and then Mike would tape the ends to the top of one of the drama department's flats. Mike and I strung every five feet from the back of the room to the front. When we had finished with just this first task, I had six rows of brightly colored, papel picado suspended overhead. Mike had helped me move my desk in front of the partition that would function as the clinic's wall, so I taped one more panel of picado, draping it every three squares for a scalloped-bunting appearance. Then, sweet Mike (what a treasure of a husband) helped me make tissue-paper flowers, replete with streamers, to tape on the walls—whether the cinderblock wall or the drama department hinged flats-as-walls. These added much-needed color, especially behind my desk.

Next, continuing our teamwork (and Mike and I do operate as a well-oiled machine, I've got to say), we hot-glued Mala's travel posters to the otherwise drab walls. We set up the easel and flip charts at what would be for me the front of the room. Since the first three weeks of Spanish I is "Oral Acquisition," I would not need a board right away. *No need to panic yet, right?* I happily discovered that Beni had also managed to find me a little bookshelf which he had set beside the ladder for me. We positioned it next to the flip charts on the easels. Mike and I unpacked my supplies from the plastic tubs and arranged all of those on the little bookcase, after I had wiped it clean of dust and cobwebs. We arranged and re-arranged desks, with me trying to decide how I wanted them so as to facilitate small-group work and take advantage of peer-tutoring techniques. Hampering our pseudo-interior design feng shui efforts was the continual problem of how to avoid the gargantuan, old equipment now shoved up against the wall with sharp-edged corners, not to even mention the several fire extinguishers attached at various points along the wall. Just as Mike and I were taking stock of what should be our next attempted configuration, an announcement blared over the loudspeaker. The gist of the announcement was to give us a thirty-minute warning that the parking lot and its entrance would be closed off and locked for more construction and that all personnel needed to begin their quick exit of the building.

"Well, Hun, it looks a hell of a lot better than it did. Guess this will have to do for now. I just will have to come early on Monday and finish organizing and decorating. Tonight, and tomorrow, you know I'm gonna have to finish work on my lesson plans, don't'cha?"

Mike nodded his weary head. "I am amazed at the strength of teachers—their mental and physical strength and their emotional fortitude. I don't think anyone outside the field would believe this."

"I don't, and I have to teach in this. What was I thinking, Mike, taking this job?"

"Swan, how could you have known? C'mon, let's go pick up the kids and get some lunch—and we'll pray that you have air conditioning, come Monday."

We locked up, walked outside into the sunshine, trying to be optimistic that Monday would be much better. Boy, were we wrong.

FIVE

First Day, First Period

Pulling into the parking lot by 7:30 a.m. with bags of tissue paper, construction paper, tape, more travel posters, and my lunch, I thought I was ready for this day. I opened the door, which opened onto Alice's side of the room, and switched on the industrial lights. *Why am I still standing here in darkness? Oh, yeah*, I remembered, as each light ever-so-slowly turned on in its own good-sweet time, each serenading me with its electrical humming (the sounds of which made my skin crawl—like fingernails on a blackboard). *Waiting, waiting, and voila! Let there be light!*

Immediately, I noticed that two of the gray flats had fallen over onto student desks on my side of the room. *Great, what if that happens while students are in class? That's a possible law suit.* The first day of classes is chaotic enough without worrying about falling flats.

As I set my bags on top of my desk, I noticed that the room was quite stuffy and warm. *Oh, well now, isn't this just dandy? The air conditioning isn't on.*

Next, I noticed an old, distressed podium that had not been here on Saturday when Mike and I had left. *Hmmm, a note's taped on top.* I read it: *Found this, thought of you. Beni.* I made a mental note to thank Beni sometime today before leaving school. Again, I thought, *custodians are a teacher's best friends.*

Quickly, I propped back up the two dividers—the drama department's flats—and straightened my students' desks. Unloading the additional posters, tape, and tissue paper, I began to rapidly slap some more color on any wall area that still looked drab. I then sat at my desk storing away items in drawers and arranging the top of my desk with necessary supply items and a few decorative ones, as well.

Nurse Mary must have already been in her clinic because I smelled the aroma of coffee coming from behind the two paneled, right-angled walls that partitioned her nurse's station from my classroom space. In front of one of those paper-thin, paneled walls, I had positioned my desk. The clinic was essentially located in one corner of the room on my side of the industrial tech space, but the worrisome part was that the clinic did not have a ceiling over its nine-foot walls. In other words, its walls (short in comparison to the twenty-foot height of the industrial tech room) were open-air to the remaining eleven feet above the paneled walls. We both knew that this was going to be interesting, indeed, for Mary had expressed to me her concern about discussing sensitive information with her clinic students without my Spanish students hearing.

"Coffee's ready!"

"Mary, you must have gotten here really early. I'd love some. Be there in a sec." I walked around the flats out of my classroom space; through Alice's drama space; out our door and turning left into our B-Hall; around the corner to the left into Main Hall going past Linzy Faith's library; around another corner to the left into D-Hall where Mala's, Jack's, and Jeb's rooms were and where Mary's doorway, next to Jeb's door, led into her small, make-shift area. The nurse's station is, in fact, within my classroom space just on the other side of those two paper-thin, paneled walls through which or over which I could just give her a 'holler-and-howdy-do' while sitting at my desk. If only we each were about ten feet tall, Mary could have just handed me a cup o'joe over the top of the paneled wall.

Mary was sitting at a small round table with two cups

of coffee. She was dressed professionally. Unlike other health professionals who wore scrubs at my previous schools, Mary wore dresses and pumps with a white medical coat—and did so consistently, I came to observe. Her salt-and-peppered hair was styled and sprayed so that every hair was always neatly in place, every black hair and every silver hair. She had been at North Gate for ten years, and for all of those ten years and since the district was small, Mary was required to travel to the elementary campus and be there from 8:00 a.m. to 11:00 a.m., but then she arrived back at the high school where she worked from 12:00 a.m. to 3:30 p.m. Over the course of several future chats, Mary revealed to me that she was divorced and that both her son and daughter were grown and married. Consequently, the North Gate faculty were her family now, and she liked taking care of us, as well as of our students, of course.

"This is nice, thank you, Mary"

"I thought you could use a good strong cup on the first day."

"Thanks. You're right. This is just what the doctor ordered."

"How's your room coming?"

"Oh, it looks a lot better. I hung decorations, called papel picado, from the ceiling, and I just finished taping travel posters to the walls. However, I'm not sure how drama and Spanish are going to work in one room. When I arrived this morning, two of Alice's two-fold, hinged flats had fallen over on top of my student desks. Can you imagine the mayhem that would cause if those things fall on the heads and backs of my students?" I blew out an exasperated puff of air. I sipped my coffee, but then gulped in the middle of a sip. "Oh! Are we gonna have any air conditioning today, ya think?"

"Nope."

"Nope—we're not, or nope—you don't know?"

"Just nope-nope, not to mention that I have to test the freshman for vision and hearing in here starting next week, and I need my students to be comfortable for that so I can get accurate readings on them." Mary sipped her coffee and then opened a can of homemade cookies. "Here, this is really what the doctor ordered. Phew! Okay, is it getting hotter or what?"

"I think it's getting hotter, yes. And, I still smell tar. Don't tell me they're working on the roof today—of all days, the first day?"

Mary nodded. "That's what I hear."

Glancing around her miniscule space, I said, "Mary, I can't believe this is your clinic. You barely have any room—what with your desk, your two file cabinets, this small round table with a couple of chairs, that cot bed, plus a small counter with sink and a half-size refrigerator! How do you even turn around in here?"

"As soon as a school board member's child or any other VIP's child is inconvenienced, that's when things will change. Until then, this is what I've got, for this year, anyway." Mary put the lid on the cookies and began rinsing out our coffee cups. "Hey, thanks for joining me."

"Oh, Mary, this was so calming. I thank you. As I'm sure you know, the first day is always crazy," I said while exiting her door.

I decided to check in on the happenings in Room 13. There sat Jeb, Jack, and Mala drinking coffee and fanning themselves with any paper or cardboard they had handy. Mala saw me and motioned with her hand for me to enter. I took a seat in a student desk. Mala was professionally dressed in a navy shirt dress with navy espadrille shoes. Both Jeb and Jack were wearing slacks, shirts, and ties. *Quite a change from their in-service attire,* I thought.

"Coffee?" Jeb was pouring his cup and refilling Mala's.

"No, thanks. Mary had coffee and cookies for me a few minutes ago."

"Ooooh, cookies, too!" Raising his cup, he made a toast. "Here's to the first day, everyone." Mala and Jeb raised their cups to join his; I raised my fist in a gesture of what I hoped would be victory over the day to come.

"Man, if I already have sweaty butt now, can you see me at the end of the day?"

"Thank you for that graphic visual image, Jack," Mala said.

Jeb rose, wiped his forehead with his coffee-stained napkin. "I'm glad I dressed up, too, so I can also sweat my ass off today. Geez!"

"See you two sweaty butts later—lunch, in here," Mala said to Jack and Jeb as they departed. Turning to me, she said, "Just like the men to complain. Here we sit, wearing panty hose, not sayin' a word. Well, Miss Swan, are you ready?"

"I think so, but I'll feel better when this first day is done. I can see hectic hours ahead of me: steering the drama students and the Spanish students to their correct sides of the room; trying to check in my students and call roll and identify the no-shows, plus add in the new-shows; explaining the course expectations; and who knows what else. To really spice up our industrial tech dual-classroom space, Alice told me that she's going to be having her students do some articulation exercises and improvisations. This first day ought to be just nifty."

Mala smiled sympathetically. "Let's meet here for lunch, Swan, and then for a few minutes after school, okay? That way, I can help if you need anything. Have a good one."

"Thanks, Mala. See you later." Fanning myself walking down B-Hall and around the corner to the right into Main Hall, suddenly, Mr. James was right in front of me, smiling.

"You look very nice," he said. "Have a good first day. Remember to watch out for those students around the equipment."

"Got it. By the way, I do have one question. In the corner of my room—well, actually, on Alice's side—is a cage crammed with old equipment—one item, for example, being a large score board. I would like to move that equipment and use that corner for a language lab. Where may I move all of that?"

"We can't move that equipment because of snakes."

I looked startled. "Did you say snakes?"

"Yes, snakes are a problem, and so we can't move out the equipment. Gotta go. 'No' to the lab."

Having shot down my idea, Mr. James turned away from me and walked to the end of Main Hall and into the cafeteria where students were registering and getting their schedules for the day. He left me standing there confused and with my jaw dropped to the floor, so to speak. *What do snakes have to do with moving an old score board?* In a stupefied daze, still pondering snakes, I rounded the corner into my B-Hall and entered the old industrial tech room to see Alice in a panic talking to Francine. Alice was obviously upset about something, easily discernible from her dramatic gesticulations.

"What's wrong, Alice? Can I help with anything?"

"Yes—well, no, but maybe. All of my drama students' schedules have the wrong room number printed on them. It's going to be absolute chaos every single class period." Alice threw up her arms in frustration, as if pleading with the twenty-foot ceiling to rain down a solution. Francine assured Alice that an announcement would be made to correct the mistake.

Do students ever really listen to those PA announcements? I suggested that we make something like street signs that would direct both sets of our students to their correct side of the room.

"Great idea," said Francine. "You and Alice get started on those, and I'll get the announcement made about room changes." Francine left us, already using her walkie-talkie to contact the school secretary as her high heels rapidly tapped down our hallway, heading no doubt outside and across the concrete courtyard plaza that led to the building housing hers and Mr. James' admin offices.

Alice sank into her chair, leaning over her desk and propping her forehead on one hand, massaging her temples.

"Okay?"

"I feel a migraine coming on. I should warn you. I'm prone to migraines."

"The first day of school is definitely a migraine kind of day. Let me know if you need help."

Once a bell had sounded, Mr. James began with announcements about room changes and, for this first day only, the bell schedule. Students hesitantly began to trickle in through our door until I had all twenty of my homeroom students. Immediately, they began to question why they had to share—as they described it—'this dirty old room with drama.' I diplomatically explained that the room would be renovated, but until then, this would be our class. Not overjoyed with my answer, they mumbled and grumbled to each other as they filled in student information cards required by the district. For this first week of school, students were to meet in homeroom for fifteen minutes at the beginning of each day. This would allow the district to disperse important information and take care of immediate schedule changes without interrupting the academic classes. We, the teachers, referred to it as 'house cleaning.' At least, this period was short and bearable.

The first period bell brought a gaggle of confused-looking students to our door. Alice and I directed them to the appropriate side of the room for each class, Theatre II and Spanish I. We were rather entertained by the looks on their faces as they scanned the large space of what had formerly been industrial technology. My twenty-five each found a desk of their choosing.

The tardy bell rang. I introduced myself en español. Mere minutes later, I heard the drama students on the other side of the two-hinged, gray, splatter-painted flats chanting in unison.

Hmmmmmmmmmm. Hmmmmmmmmmm.
Ha, Ha, Ha, Ha.
Guh, Guh, Guh, Guh.
Pah, Pah, Pah, Pah.
Buh, Buh, Buh, Buh.
A tutor who tooted the flute,
Tried to tutor two tooters to toot.
Said the two to the tutor,
"Is it easier to toot,
Or to tutor two tooters to toot?"
Hmmmmmmmmmm. Hmmmmmmmmmm.

Articulation practice? This must be that activity that Alice mentioned she intended to use with her first-period students in Theatre Arts II. My Spanish students wasted no time in protesting. Hands shot up all around me, flying wildly to grab my attention.

"Miss, we can't hear you with all that noise they're making!"

"Yeah, Miss! Why do they have to be in our room, anyway, huh?"

"What are they even talking about over there?"

"They're stupid, that's what they're sayin'!

Sigh.

Give me the gift of a grip-top sock,
A clip drape shipshape tip top sock.
Not your spin slick slapstick slipshod stock,
But a plastic, elastic grip-top sock.
None of your fantastic slack swap slop...

While I recognized and appreciated this Dr. Seuss rhyme as much as anyone, I had to think fast of a way to help my Spanish students be able to drown out the drama students' noise and hear and concentrate on what I needed to say to them. "Okay, kids, let's all get into a tight circle on the floor so we can better hear each other. Now, listen up. I need you to pass in your info cards as soon as you get settled in the circle."

From a slap dash flash cash haberdash shop.
Not a knick knack knitlock knock-kneed knick-
erbocker sock

"Miss, I'm wearing my new outfit. My mother will kill me if I get it dirty. I am not going to sit on this grimy, grungy floor, Miss!"

"Fine, then—uh, what's your name?"

"Haley."

"Fine, then, Haley, you may sit on top of one of the desks right behind our circle. Is anyone else worried about their clothing?" Someone else was also refusing to sit on the floor.

"Yes, what's your name?"

"Stan."

"He's our star athlete, Miss," someone offered helpfully.

"I'm worried about my designer jeans. These cost me a month's worth of allowance, Miss."

> Nothing slipshod drip drop flip flop or glip glop
> Tip me to a tip top grip top sock.

"Stan, do what Haley's doing; sit on one of the desks back there. Are we good now?" *Oh, my goodness. I'm going to get one of Alice's migraines if this keeps up all day.* I tried to begin again, this time by explaining the course outline and my grading procedures. A hand went up. I knew whose it was now, at least. "Yes, Haley?"

"What's that smell?"

"Men are working on the roof over D-Hall. That smell is tar, but it will go away soon. *I hope.* Please try to ignore it, Haley."

"Miss, I promise I'm going to throw up if I have to smell this all day."

"Okay. Let's just take things slowly. If you have to cover your nose, please do so." No sooner had I made that recommendation to Haley when, one-by-one, each of my students started covering his or her noses. *Oh, Lord, help me.* This is shades of teacher in-service last week.

I continued with the rest of the basic, general class information. That left only five minutes to teach my students introductions in Spanish. With the drama students doing their chanting thing in the background, this very simple lesson of mine became a challenge because my students were still having difficulty hearing each other and me. They, and I, were growing increasingly frustrated. Moreover, I noticed it was getting hotter by the minute and, of course, how could I forget that Linzey Faith had warned about the no air conditioning situation, which Nurse Mary had confirmed to me this morning over coffee. *The heat, plus the noxious odor of tar, is going to make for a challenging first day—and it's only first period.* I asked, "Class, are you getting too hot?"

My entire class moaned, "Yes, Miss!"

"I'm sorry, but that can lead into learning our first word today: 'ventilador.' Repeat after me, ven-ti-la-dor."

In unison, the class repeated, " Ven-ti-la-dor."

"Can anyone guess what a ventilador is?" Silence. Turning to the butcher paper taped to the wall to simulate a chalkboard, I wrote the word for my students to see it. Again, I asked, "Can anyone guess now?" I spied one hand in the air. "Yes, sí, you—what's your name? ¿Cómo se llama?"

"Taylor. My name's Taylor. Does it mean a 'ventilator,' Miss?"

Another raised his hand. It belonged to Stan the star athlete. "Car vent?"

"Good connection—both of you! What does a ventilator or a car vent do?"

Taylor and Stan looked at each other, perhaps for confidence. "Circulate air?" Stan said.

"Excellent! So what is a ventilador?" Silence, again. Using gestures, I began fanning myself.

"Oh, oh, oh! A fan!" Everybody seemed to respond together—now that the lightbulb had clicked on in their minds.

"¡Olé, clase!. You're so smart that there's no homework for tonight." The students slapped each other's hands in victory. (Of course, there was not going to be any home work for this first day, but I preferred to let them think that they had earned a reward.) Finally, the dismissal bell rang, ending first period. I wished them well on their first day for the rest of the day.

We were all going to need well-wishes to get through this first day. I thought to myself, *Sweaty butts, tar, snakes, and tutor-toot drills—oh, my! What will the rest of this day bring?*

SIX

First Day, Rest of Day

Second period—same as first—except more and more students were becoming ill from the heat and the smell of tar. Julie the cheerleader asked to go to the clinic as she thought she might vomit. I wrote a pass and gave Julie directions on how to get there. A few seconds later, I heard a loud, exclamatory cry: "Miss help, I didn't make it."

I ran to help Julie. Meanwhile, Alice's drama students were making their own exclamatory shrieks, jumping out of their seats, and scurrying to a corner of Alice's space to get as far away from the smell and sight of vomit as possible.

"Alice, would you please call Beni for a cleanup?" Our only walkie-talkie, held in its charging port, was on her side of the room. "I'll take Julie to the clinic. Would you also keep an eye on my students?" Alice nodded as she grabbed for the walkie-talkie.

I hollered to Mary, pitching my voice over the short paneled wall: "Nurse Mary, a student has become ill in my class; I'm going to walk her over to you." Mary must have immediately called for Francine to meet me with the ill student, whom she escorted to the main office to wait there for a parent to come and get her.

Meanwhile, my Spanish students evidently had joined Alice's drama students because when I returned, I saw that they were all huddled together in the corner while Beni was mopping up the vomit. Upon entering, I heard a cacophony of complaints.

"Ooooooh, yuk!"

"Upchuck yuk!"

"Peee-yew!"

"Gag me with ten spoons!"

"Miss, I may throw up, too!"

I walked over to Alice to whisper in her ear, "I'm going to take my group outside; do you want to join us?" Alice gave a thumbs up in agreement.

Both classes filed outside to the courtyard. My Spanish students sat in circle on one side of the plaza, and Alice's drama students sat in a circle on the other side. Thank goodness, no one complained about ruining their clothes by sitting on the concrete. We did the best we could to hold the students' attention as we each covered our course information. Sometimes, however, the temptation of waving to random classmates who, now and then, were traversing from one building to another must have been too great for our students to resist. I didn't fight it. After all, it was only the first day.

Third period study hall was blissfully uneventful, thank goodness. In-between second and third periods, Beni had brought us two big fans to help us, we all hoped, contend against the tar smell and the heat. This third period was a study hall that didn't require teaching or course expectations. It was a 'catch-my-breath time' so as to gear up for the afternoon's classes.

Fourth period would be my conference. Fifth period was going to be my lunch. *Whew! If I can just hold on and make it to lunch.* It would be then that Mala and I would meet in room 13 to touch base with each other.

During my fourth-period conference, I went to the copy room at the back of the library where our teachers' boxes were located. As all teachers are expected to do throughout the school day, whenever possible,

I had to check my box for any updated information. Entering the library, I waved to Linzey Faith.

"I hear you have had a fun day thus far." Linzey Faith gave her impish grin. Today, she was dressed in a black pencil skirt and white blouse with tiny seed-pearl buttons. Her long, brown hair was pulled back in a pony tail. Because Linzey Faith must have been chilled in her air-conditioned library, she wore an orange, crocheted sweater over her blouse.

"Nice sweater, Linzey Faith, but I assure you that if you go into A, B, C, and D-hallways and classrooms, you won't need that."

"Told you," Linzey Faith said. "We shall be without air conditioning for today and tomorrow. By the way, I certainly hope you do not need to copy anything. The machine is down."

"Gosh, you are just full of good news today."

Linzey Faith sang out her response. "Glad I could help!"

As I made my way back to the teachers' boxes, I could hear Linzey Faith begin giving instructions to a group of students who had just arrived to do a first-day assignment that would introduce them to the layout of the library and a refresher on the Dewey decimal system. Passing the library's large bulletin board, I saw that Linzey Faith had decorated it quite nicely for the start of the school year. However, once at the teachers' mailboxes, something caught my eye on the little faculty bulletin board back in the copy room. The 'something' was a drawing of Mala and me donned in our protective helmets. Beside it was an original drawing, compliments of Jeb. I silently mouthed the caption: *New Safety Team. Run!* Jeb—ever the jokester, I was learning—never missed an opportunity to poke fun at his colleagues.

Going through my box, I threw away everything except a new bell schedule and an updated set of class rolls, and then headed back through the library. I was surprised to hear Mala's voice. Pausing to listen for a minute, I heard her telling a humorous narrative, using Spanish, about a student who fell asleep in class. *This must be Spanish III,* I thought. *Guess the smell got to them and Mala decided to relocate her class; don't blame her.*

With my eyes scanning the library, I located her and her class. *Huh, her navy dress looks about a foot and a half shorter; wonder why?* Mala was moving enthusiastically from table to table, sometimes standing on chairs to use each as a mini-stage while telling her imaginative story. Out of the corner of my eye, I saw Linzey Faith walk around out from behind her circulation desk and take a hands-on-hips stance. *Uh-oh. She does not approve of Mala standing on her library chairs, not one bit.* Mala took me by surprise when she spotted me by suddenly pitching the story over to me at a point where the fictional student had fallen asleep in class and was dreaming, instead of listening to the teacher. Picking up the reins (in Spanish, of course), I quickly inserted that the dreaming student saw a vision of his teacher as a strange, multi-eyed creature. Because Mala stayed silent, I added one more detail— that the dreamer felt a classmate begin to shake his arm. However, Mala jumped back in and further described half-bird/half-lizard, pantomiming with almost wild abandon the physicality of such a teacher-creature from atop her perch on one of the chairs. Just as the snickering students were beginning to find the idea humorous, the bell rang to end fourth period. Mala's students groaned. They really had gotten caught up in the story and were genuinely disappointed to have to leave.

"Real quickly, class, before you leave: Your homework for tomorrow is to draw and write a description, en español, of an 'alebrije.' Alebrijes are indigenous art forms," Mala continued, "that combine characteristics of three different animals and are brightly painted. Now, some people are convinced that these don't exist, but using your vivid imagination, I suspect that you will discover that they just might. With the help of all of you, our room will have a wall full of alebrijes." Mala grinned her biggest grin while extending a victorious thumbs-up gesture to Linzey Faith, who then pouted and sauntered away from the circulation desk where she had been standing. The students filed out of the library and on to their next class period and/or lunch period.

I giggled and said, "Ready for lunch? I'll meet you in Room 13. Oh, and hey! What's up with your dress?"

"I was getting over heated in my room, so I used duct tape to hem it about a foot shorter. I'm thinking about selling the idea. What do you think?"

"I say—keep your day job."

"You're no fun. See ya in a bit. I've got to check my box, too."

Once Mala, Jeb, Jack, and I were all seated at a table in Room 13 and nibbling on our various lunch items, our chitchat eventually devolved into a pity-party complaint-fest about having been so pressed for time that morning. To change the subject, Mala said, "Okay, folks. I've had two students throw up in the clinic due to the tar smell and heat." Jeb reported that his students had been fine thus far, but then Jack said that he had had to send Haley, complaining of nausea, to the clinic.

"Haley with the red hair?" I asked.

"Yes, do you have her?"

"I do, first period. In my class this morning, she griped about the condition of the room, then about the tar smell—so, she did get sick?"

"Apparently, on the way to the clinic. Poor Mary. I hear all she's been doing this morning is help quell the uneasy stomachs of our barfing students."

I gave more of an account of the first half of my day. "First period, we all—with our noses covered, mind you—sat on the floor in a tight circle just to be able to try and hear each other over all the noise that drama was making. Second period, I had to take my class outside because one of my students got sick in my room—well, actually, on Alice's side of our room. After that, Beni brought us some big fans which helped with the tar and vomit smell, at least. However, the noise from the drama students' articulation drills was outrageously disruptive to my Spanish class, almost to the point of being comical, only not. Still, I understand that Alice must teach her class in our space, too. I just don't see how this little arrangement is going to work."

"You're right, it's gonna be challenging," Mala said. "I bet Alice thinks so, as well, don't you?" I nodded as I took a big gulp of my iced tea, then a bite of my salad. "So, how did your next class go? Tell us."

" Third period was uneventful, thank goodness. Oh, and by the way," I glanced around the table, "I noticed a little something thumb-tacked up on the library's bulletin board—a certain drawing was on display?" I raised my pitch on that last word, along with one of my eyebrows, and peered teasingly at Jeb. "Wonder where that came from, huh, Jeb?"

Suddenly, Francine appeared in Mala's doorway and asked to speak with me. I joined her in the hall, carrying my tea with me. Francine explained that Alice was having one of her migraines and that she could not stay with her class right now, as she needed to go lie down in the clinic for a little while. Francine asked if I could possibly finish lunch in the next few minutes and go watch the drama students. "Sure, but what do I do when my Spanish II class comes sixth period?"

"I'll come back at that point and by then, we will work something out, I promise." Francine spun away from me with her heels making sharp taps as she made her way down D-Hall and around the corner into Main Hall, heading to mine and Alice's room in B-Hall, I figured. "Thanks, trust me it is not always like this," Francine said to me over her shoulder.

I walked back to our make-shift lunch table, grabbed my salad container, and stabbed one more bite to eat before snapping the lid shut on the disposable container and tossing it in Mala's trash can.

"You already in trouble the first day?" asked Jack.

"No, apparently, Alice has a migraine, and Francine says my services are needed now. I'm out guys. Later." I exited with at least the rest of my iced tea.

As I entered, I saw Beni the wonderful janitor sitting at Alice's desk. *This man does everything.* I informed Beni that I was there to relieve him, so that he could be on his way (certain he had work of his own that was waiting for him). I sat with Alice's students the remaining few minutes of what had been my lunch period. Shortly, the bell rang for sixth period. One set of students left, and a new set began entering—both mine and Alice's.

As they did so, I said sufficient times for them all to hear my message, "Okay, guys, everybody over here on the drama side. We're going to combine classes this period. Get in one big circle on the stage." Once they were all settled, I continued. "Let's start by introducing ourselves, and I want you each to share one neat thing you did during the summer. I'll go first. My name is Mrs. Jones. I had a beach vacation; my husband and I spent time this summer at South Padre Island."

One by one, the students were sharing their summer activities when, suddenly, the PA system popped. Over the loud speaker, Mr. James' voice interrupted one of the students. He made an announcement about athletic schedules for seventh and eighth periods. Once he finished, the dismissal bell rang ending sixth period. *Two more to go,* I thought.

I sighed with relief, but wondering what else could possibly happen on this first day, as I walked over to my side of the industrial tech room space to greet my seventh period Spanish II students as they arrived. Alice walked through our doorway slowly, gave a weak wave to acknowledge me, and then sat down at her desk. *At least she's back. Whew. That's one less worrisome detail.*

The tardy bell rang for seventh period, and I began my intro speech for the fifth time. Within ten minutes, I heard the drama students begin reciting their articulation drills, obviously working on their projection, as well. Once again, I instructed my students to form a circle on the floor so they could better hear the rest of my lesson, but of course, right away, a hand shot up in the air. It belonged to a student named Katie. She, as others of my students before her on this first day, was protesting about being asked to sit on the floor because she did not want to get her new outfit dirty. I suggested that she sit on top of a desk behind the circle and lean in to hear.

As Katie was positioning herself on top of a desk, another hand flew up. I asked this student's name; he told me it was Coop. I remembered that during roll call, he had established his name to be this, short for Cooper. Coop was tall, lanky, and rather spunky (or was it goofy?). From later conversations with faculty, I learned that Coop had the reputation of being the class clown. He wasted no time in establishing that reputation in my seventh-period Spanish class on this first day.

"Miss, look! Kay-Kay is molting. Look, look!"

"Cooper, I beg your pardon?"

"Coop! It's Coop, Miss. Call me Coop!"

"My apologies, Coop. Now, clear up my confusion, please. What on earth are you talking about?"

"Look at her legs—she's molting!"

The class caught on before I did. A wave of snickering circulated our circle as all eyes were upon Katie's legs that dangled from where she sat atop a desk. I looked, too. Katie's hosiery—her stockings—were quite loose and very much collapsed into wrinkles around her ankles.

"Coop, you're so mean. Miss, I can't keep these things up." I motioned for Katie to meet me outside in the hallway. I could hear her sliding footsteps as she followed me. Once I made it to our hall just outside the classroom door, I looked to see how far behind me she was. The drama students had all but dropped their jaws in a silent, communal pause as they gawked at the shuffling-step Katie, who had grabbed each stocking at the knees and was valiantly making the effort to try and hold them up as she traipsed awkwardly past the dramatic articulation drills.

"Katie, are you wearing panty hose?"

"No, Miss. They're the separate kind."

"Do you have a garter belt or something to keep them up?"

"No, I thought they just stayed up on their own. I've had the hardest day, Miss! I've been having to hold these darn things up all day."

"Katie, I recommend that you go to the restroom and take them off for the last two class periods. Those are meant to be worn with a garter belt or something. That has to be hard trying to walk around campus like that." She nodded dolefully at my commiseration toward her. Leaving Katie in the hallway, I walked to my desk and wrote out a pass for the restroom. "Here, go to the restroom; take those off and just ball them up in your hand. Hurry back to class, and then you can stuff them in your purse, maybe."

"Thank you, Miss."

Walking back into the room, I asked my students to pass in their index-information cards. Amidst the loud, whirring hum of the circulating fans and the crisply-articulated chants of the drama students, I proceeded to go over course expectations. As with all of my earlier classes, just as I began my "Lesson 1: Introduction in Spanish," the dismissal bell rang.

One more, only one more class. Can I make it through this crazy first day? What else can possibly happen? I had been through vomiting; covering another teacher's class during the last part of what should have been my time to decompress a little bit—my lunch period; covering two different classes of two entirely different subjects simultaneously; sweating students; stinky tar; and just a few minutes earlier, molting. *Just another day in the paradise of a teacher's world.*

Eighth hour, finally—and thanks to the student grapevine, by now most of the students could easily find their side of this old industrial tech room that Alice and I (not to forget, to a lesser extent, Nurse Mary) now had to call our classroom home. Alice had informed me during the passing period as we stood in our hallway to greet our last batch of students that no 'artic drills' would be done during this last period because these would be her middle-school students. *Thank goodness for small miracles. That'll be nice—nice to have her students and mine be able to actually sit in their desks for once this first day!*

As my students were filling in their index-information cards, the drama students began to rearrange their desks in order to get ready for some kind of role-play activity that I overheard Alice introducing to them. I waited for their noises of scraping, dragged desks to cease; then, I began going over course expectations, pausing occasionally to ask if any of my students had questions or comments. Eighth hour proceeded rather blissfully calm with my Spanish II students being quite cooperative. This was mainly because they had heard similar information from their teachers in their other classes and, by now, they were too hot and too tired to care about anything. As I concluded the explanation of grading procedures, I paused for questions; my numbed, tired students sat passively silent, mentally napping.

"Oh, no! Look out!" someone shouted. One of the hinged, two-fold gray flats toppled onto the back row of my students because a middle schooler, hunched into a cardboard box (cut out and painted to resemble a red car), along with several other middle schoolers pushing the contraption at top speed (for a cardboard box, that is), crashed into my side of the room. The effected, back-row Spanish students hopped up and quickly leaped out of the way. The 'driver,' along with the several who were essentially his engine, collapsed in peals of raucous laughter on top of each other—and on top of the gray flat. All the students were shrieking in delight at this unexpected entertainment; I tried clapping my hands to bring order out of chaos; and Alice had a horrified look on her face as she ran over to check on her youngsters.

"I am so sorry! Is everyone okay?" Alice asked.

"I think that they're all fine, Ms. Simmons," I said. "Will some of my students please help Ms. Simmons set her flat back up in place?" They did; the hinged, two-sided flat once again stood upright—a testament to valiantly surviving the red cardboard car crash of eighth period. *Oh, great, just great. The drama students and the Spanish students will now be able to see each other through the two big rips in the spatter-painted muslin fabric. I hope Alice has another one to use in its place.*

"We're fine, Miss! That was awesome!" squealed Alice's little motorists as she scurried them back to her side of the room with her apologies directed to me over her shoulder. My students concurred. They were all fine, just fine and dandy.

"Hey! Everyone okay in there?" yelled Mary through the paneling that only thinly separated her nurse's station from Alice's and my jointly-shared classroom space.

"No injuries, Nurse Mary," I said as I walked back to the front of my side of the room to address my Spanish students. "Well, that was certainly an exciting way to end the day; most important, though, do any of you have questions about the course?" The students shook their heads 'no.' The bell rang to end eighth period. I wished them well; reminded them about homeroom in the morning; and dismissed them.

The last of my students left. I sank into my chair. I put my head down on the desk. *No one except my colleagues in Room 13 would believe the day I've had. No one.*

Several minutes later, I mustered up enough energy to walk to Room 13, despite my feet feeling like leaden dead weights as I struggled to lift each one. *Just put one foot in front of the other.* I needed to be able to commiserate with my fellow front-line teacher-warriors.

Mala was a sight for sore eyes. She sat in a student desk

with her feet propped up, shoes off, duct-taped hem, and fanning herself with the day's bell schedule. "Swan, you look as bad as I feel," Mala said as I walked into the room.

"Please tell me I am dreaming and will wake up," I said as I sank into another student desk across from her and buried my head in my hands.

"Well, this is a picture worth a thousand words." Jack poked his head in the door. "Are we tired, ladies?"

"Go away, Jack, if you value your life," Mala and I said in unison. He chuckled with a wave as he walked on past Mala's door.

Two cups of coffee arrived in Jeb's hands. "Thought you two could probably use some of this right about now." In a teasing tone, Jeb said, " I heard about the car crash in eighth period, Mrs. Jones."

"Car crash?" Mala asked. "Was there a wreck on campus today?"

Snickering wearily, I said, "No, the 'wreck' was in my room. One of the middle school drama students, driving (I made 'air quotations' here) a cardboard car painted fire engine red and which was being pushed by several other giggling middle schoolers, came crashing into my side of the class. Plowing straight into one of Alice's two-sided flats, all accident victims toppled on top of each other in even more uproarious giggling. Luckily no one was hurt—only Alice's flat. Can't you just hear that story around dinner tables tonight?"

Mala erupted in laughter; I caught hers; it was infectious because Jeb joined us in a good-old-fashioned belly laugh—tears running down our cheeks, pounding a desk, slapping a knee, doubled over in that kind of extended laughter that comes from great exhaustion. As soon as one would stop laughing, another would get tickled, and it would start all over again. Like a foghorn, our laughter must have caused Jack to do a U-turn in the hallway and come back to Room 13 and lure Linzey Faith from her library. They poked their heads in to see what was so funny. I tried to tell the story again, but then a new wave of laughter boiled up and spilled over, so Mala and Jeb would try to pick up the pieces of my story until laughter overtook their speech, and I'd have to try and convey another snippet of the tale of the cardboard car. *A merry heart doeth good like a medicine*, suddenly recalling that Bible verse, I felt refreshed.

"Here, I brought the latest bell schedules from your boxes." Linzey Faith handed Mala and I each a Xeroxed copy.

"Another one, geez," Mala sighed.

"By the way Mala, we don't stand on chairs in the library."

"Sorry, Linz. That library rule must have slipped my mind.

"Can't you let anything go?" asked Jack. With that, he exited again.

"My library, my rules. And Jean, please call me Linzey Faith. That is my name."

Spinning with a degree of disgruntlement, Linzey Faith Reinerd exited Room 13.

"Alright, gang, we're on over-time. See you all tomorrow." Jeb excused himself from our little after-school fiesta as he had to set up a lab for tomorrow's class.

Mala and I looked at each other and started laughing again. "It's like kindergarten here, isn't it? How do you survive this, Mala?"

"I just make it meaningful for the students; they're the reason we're here. You want to know what really helps me?" I nodded. "I live outside of town on a farm that I call El Ranchito. After a day like today, I go home; sit in a rocker on the back porch; sip my iced tea; and watch the barn cats fuck." Exploding out my mouth, the coffee that I had just sipped splattered all over the desktop. I leaned over to snatch a Kleenex from a box that Mala had on her teacher desk and quickly mopped up the liquid. As Mala continued, I was all ears. "I try to relax and let the day go because tomorrow will be another day, and each day brings its own stuff. Gotta get ready for the next day's stuff, Swan." Mala, giving me a playful wink and a smile, took another sip of her coffee.

I rose to go throw away the soppy Kleenex in Mala's trash can by her door. "That was just what the doctor ordered—a laugh-fest! Mala, you are the only reason I will survive this crazy year."

"I know, Kiddo."

"Oh, I've got one for you; I almost forgot. The language lab idea is a no-go. Mr. James said snakes are a problem."

"Wait a minute—were those his exact words? That doesn't make any sense, but then, when does he ever make sense!"

"Good, I thought I was losing it, or that I had missed the part of our in-service agenda about snakes."

"Sounds like an underground project to me. We'll tackle that one later. For now, let's go home while we can still move. The good news about today is that it's officially over."

SEVEN

Cages, Britches, & Stitches

After the first three weeks of teaching at my new school, I was still in survival mode. While clinging tenaciously to the high ideals of an educator, I had to maneuver through or dodge the random and unpredictable grenades of disorder. I simply was trying to manage chaos.

I didn't want to remain in survival mode, though. Somehow, some kind of way, I needed to eventually turn this environment around so that I was not the one being acted upon as a helpless bystander. Instead, I needed to act upon this environment and circumstances (for my own sanity) in order to transform it into a more positive and definitely more productive situation. I needed to grab the bull by the horns—but first, I had to catch the bull. I needed to grasp the full extent of 'the problem' so that I could better devise 'the solution.'

To that end, my crazy compadres and I would meet every morning in Room 13 before hall duty to commiserate about any shenanigans of the day before. There, we encouraged each other; revved up our motors; recharged our batteries for the day ahead; and brainstormed, brainstormed, brainstormed to try and problem-solve the discombobulated bedlam in which we found ourselves. We began to call these gatherings the 'Breakfast Club.' During this preposterous year, Jeb's coffee kept my spirits high, and Mala kept me sane.

More craziness ensued as the year progressed. Dealing with the plethora of whack-a-doodle situations became the norm—more months of the first year than I care to remember. Unfortunately, I do remember.

First, I remember Mr. James' responses bordering on being dry and sarcastic if not downright ridiculous when asking him about moving all that equipment stored in my room and in the cages on Alice's side ('Snakes are a problem'); when asking about his promise of a chalkboard and an overhead projector ('What are you going to give me?'); and inquiring about a locking cabinet to secure my purse and test materials ('Just don't give tests'). Stopping about ten steps after passing him in the hall and asking him my questions, I would think, *Wait a minute, what did he just say?*

After Labor Day, I secretly went forward with the language lab without his approval (but in cahoots with Beni). One Saturday, my husband and I sneaked into the building. Quickly and quietly, we moved the scoreboard—the biggest obstacle—to one of the other cages containing even more equipment. (Beni had conveniently left the chain-locked doors to the cages open.) Then, Mike and I rearranged a metal table against the wall of the single cleared-out cage; hung the headphones on tag board; and added three old, metal, industrial chairs. The mission was accomplished in one hour.

Excitedly, I showed Mala our new language lab the next Monday. She said, "It's perfect! Can't wait until Mr. James finds it."

"I can. How am I going to spin this?"

"With answers like his, Swan. Answers that aren't really answers."

Sure enough, one afternoon in October while heading over to Room 13, I heard, "Mrs. Jones, I need to ask you a question." I stopped in my tracks and turned to face Mr. James.

"Okay, what is it, Sir?"

"I noticed one of those cages has been cleaned out and there seems to be a language lab there now."

"Really?" I gave him my best, confused look.

"Did you move that equipment and that big scoreboard out of one of those cages?"

"I did not, Sir." Technically, that was not a lie because my husband had moved the huge scoreboard and all the other equipment so that I could have plausible deniability. The clueless look on his face was priceless.

Mala and I were both surprised that our principal never again brought up the topic of the language lab; moreover, he didn't order me to take it down, either. This was a win-win situation, as Mala and I saw it. Our students loved doing lab activities in our clandestine lab. Furthermore, over time, Mala and I realized that Mr. James had never actually been opposed to the language lab, per se; what had actually worried him had more to do with where to store all that massive, extra equipment (and who was going to do the physical labor of moving it). The campus storage facility was full to the gills, which meant that the industrial tech equipment would have had to be stored either outside the maintenance shed or outside some other campus building—not only visible to the public, but also providing a warm and cozy hiding place for those South Texas snakes. We had taken care of his concerns.

Second, I remember the concerns that Nurse Mary, Alice, and I all had regarding the clinic having no ceiling of its own but, instead, being open-air above its nine-foot paneled walls with only the twenty-foot industrial-type ceiling high overhead. Without a ceiling over the nurse's station, both Alice's and my classes were at least vaguely aware of what all transpired in there between nurse and patient. This surely violated privacy and confidentiality of the students but also the occasional faculty or staff member who needed the nurse's services.

One especially memorable incident exemplified a recurring problem: the nurse's station (and Mary, of course) were needed for students with disabilities to clean up (or to be helped in cleaning up) or to change clothes (or to be helped in changing clothes) after "accidents." Those accidents that were par for the course for some of our special needs students went somewhat unnoticed by the rest of us. Those accidents due to illness, however, were impossible to politely ignore.

One day in November while teaching conjugations to seventh period, I noticed a strong, unpleasant smell. A few minutes later, I overheard the special education assistant explaining to Robbie, one of his wheelchair-bound students, that he needed to help Robbie change his soiled clothes.

Robbie announced, rather loudly, "Dia-ruh.'

"Yes, Robbie. You've got diarrhea. We'll get you all cleaned up, though."

The odor became so noxious that my students had to clasp their hands over their noses, nodding their heads in the direction of the clinic (as if I couldn't smell the problem). "Miss, what is that?" asked Coop.

Trying to preserve Robbie's dignity, I tilted my head in the direction of the clinic and put my finger over my mouth to silence the class. When Katie started gagging, though, I motioned for my students to exit the room quietly. As we walked past Alice's class, I noticed her students were all huddled in the corner surrounding her in her desk and registering their complaints, as well. Not long after we had exited the building for some fresh air in the courtyard, Alice's class followed suit. For thirty minutes, Alice and I tried our best to occupy our own students; we also encouraged them not to embarrass Robbie by talking about this incident with others.

Of course, within five seconds of the bell ringing that

ended seventh period, I heard Coop shouting as he reentered our building to go to his next class, "Hey, Boomer! Spanish got to have class outside because Robbie shit in his pants again."

Katie issued forth her promise as she exited our courtyard classroom, "If my things still smell like poop in my next class, my mama and daddy are gonna sue this school."

Like rain splattering on mud, the comments continued to fall and carry over into eighth period. After such 'odorous invasions,' Beni would come and spray air freshener in an attempt to disguise the smell, but the odor would always linger for hours, even sometimes into the next day. Alice and I had to exit our room four more times that year due to these odorous illness invasions.

December finally arrived and by now, I was in good spirits because Christmas break was two weeks away. Cooler weather, an old overhead projector that Linzey Faith had loaned me, and Secret Santa diverted my attention from the day-to-day challenges of teaching in the industrial tech room with drama classes.

Oh, a much needed reprieve was that Christmas break! It energized me to start the new semester, yet once back at school, I was already thinking, *Come on summer.*

As is typical in public school education, the second semester usually starts with in-service meetings and a teacher work day. This back-to-school January in-service session was just more curriculum planning. *Yadda yadda yadda and bla bla bla. Same song, second verse.*

The only thing good about in-service days is that teachers get to leave campus to go eat lunch at restaurants. After a two-week break, I was eager to catch up with my colleagues. I had missed my Breakfast Club friends and was excited to hear all of their holiday stories.

January and February flew by like a dream—a bad dream—with the noise of dual-teaching for different subjects in what had formerly been the cavernous industrial tech classroom space now delineated into two classroom areas by flats that toppled over on an almost daily basis. From over the nurse's paneled wall-with-no-ceiling still floated the sounds of diarrhea splats and the occasional vomiting and moaning and conversations that, once heard, cannot be un-heard.

Third and finally, as one more example of this first year at my new school, I remember at mid-spring the plan to have a one-day in-service, only this time with a guest consultant brought all the way in from Maine. Her name was Margaret. *Margaret from Maine.*

This expenditure was deemed necessary by Karen,

the district's curriculum director. One Friday morning, Karen marched into Alice's and my room to inform us that the district wanted to use it for Monday's session.

Alice and I blinked at each other and said in unison, "You want to use this room?"

"Yes. I'm thinking that you, Elizabeth, could just move all your students' desks up against the wall and maybe shove your teacher desk and bookcase up against that paneled wall. Alice, you could stack your student desks on top of Elizabeth's; and then, if you two would move these dividers over in front of all the desks to kind of conceal them, that would be great. That should give us enough space for a tripod screen, a computer on an AV cart for power point presentations, and all the tables and chairs that Beni can then move in here for all the faculty."

I was still stuck back on the word 'just.' When I found my voice again, I said, "So, Karen, you want Alice and me to basically shove each of our classroom items against the wall? Are you going to help, or at least provide us with some help, for this little chore? Today is Friday, you know that, Karen, right?".

"Can't you get some students to help you?" (I wanted to wipe that patronizing smirk off her face; she had said that remark in a tone and manner insinuating that

I obviously must have forgotten that we have students.)

"On a Friday, Karen? Are you aware how students bolt out of here like lightning on Fridays?"

"Oh, alright. I hadn't thought about that. Don't worry, I'll find someone to help you before the day is over." She made that her exit line. (*Famous last words*, I thought.)

"Hmmm, Alice?"

"Yes, Elizabeth?"

"Whom do you think besides poor, put-upon Beni that Karen will con into helping us?"

"I dunno. I do know that Beni will have enough of his own burden of tables and chairs to move into here, so I don't think that I will hold my breath."

At lunch in Room 13, I shared the last-minute news about our upcoming in-service being slated for the in-dustrial tech room.

"Ah, you see, Liz, you over-decorated with all those piña colada thingeys. You should have left it old and dusty."

"Those thingeys are papel picado," I said, correcting Jeb.

"Still, what were you thinking?"

"That Alice and I had to live in that place all year, and that by at least adding color with the papel picado and travel posters and—"

"So let me get this straight," Jack interrupted. "Karen tells you today, on a Friday, that the entire faculty is going to be meeting in your room on Monday, but first you and Alice have to move and stack all your student desks against a wall and out of the way. Also you must move your books and bookcase and teacher desks out of the way; plus drag the two-fold flats in front of what will be a pyramid of desks. Finally, you have to get this done pronto so that Beni can set up tables and chairs in there either this afternoon or evening or tomorrow or early Monday morning? And all this work for a one-day in-service that the district is spending wa-doodles on to fly in some cockamamie curriculum specialist from Maine all the way here to South Texas? And then you and Alice will have to set up your room spaces again late Monday when this party's all over? Am I to understand that correctly?"

"My room and Alice's will be basically squashed against the wall. That is correct, Sir."

"Why the hell can't we hold this shindig in the cafeteria where we normally have faculty meetings?"

"Jack, I've asked around. Seems that the district coaches are having an all-day meeting in the cafeteria," I said.

"So why the hell not the damn library, then? 'Scuse me, Linzey Faith."

"I can answer that one for you, Elizabeth," said Linzey Faith. "Jack, for your information, the full-faculty curriculum in-service cannot be in my library as the district's counselors will be spreading out their spring testing materials on many of my tables, and they will be collating those testing materials according to test function and by grade level and class. That is why, Jack."

"Well, la-te-dah," said Jack. "I stand rebuked by Miss Reinerd.

"And who gets to help you with this fun chore?" Mala finally chimed in, and I was glad because she kind of broke the tension between Jack and Linzey Faith. "And does Karen know that those flats fall over almost daily?"

"It's not like I can say no."

Mala said, "This is just plain bad. The gall of admin to expect this of you and Alice. I'm so sorry, Swan. What I'm really sorry about is that I can't stay and help you this afternoon. Bob and I promised our daughter we'd come visit her this weekend for some parents' day function this evening and tomorrow at the university. We have to head out of town right after school."

Jeb said he urgently needed to clean up from his labs today; do some lesson planning and grading of tests; and then set up for labs on Tuesday, since he would not have the time late Monday after the in-service to do all that.

"Maybe this will work to your advantage," Jack said. "Maybe that Yankee consultant and our dear district curriculum specialist will be amazed that you and Alice have to teach in that crap environment, sharing the space not only with each other but with all that dusty, dirty, big-honkin' machinery they're still storing in there."

"I hope so. All I know is it will be very interesting. Hey, if I don't see you all after school—and I probably won't as I believe that I'll be a bit busy—have a great week-end, everybody."

As I was leaving Room 13, Jack hollered at me, "Oh, and by the way, Elizabeth," I stopped in Mala's doorway to turn and look at him. "Sorry, but I promised my grandson that I'd be at his soccer match this afternoon, or you know I'd come and help ya, Kid."

"Thanks, Jack. This is not your problem. Alice and I and

Beni will somehow get it done. See ya later, gang."

I walked back to class to finish the afternoon. Minutes before the bell to dismiss eighth period, an office aide came to my side of the room with a message from Karen. It read:

> Don't forget we are using your room. Please make sure you move all your desks. See you Monday.
>
> Karen

(I love how she provided that help she promised.)

As soon as the bell rang and my last student had exited, I began shoving each and every student desk, along with the rest of my entire classroom, against the cinderblock wall. That also included my having to unload books from my bookcase so that it would be light enough for me to drag over and position against the paneled wall that I shared with Nurse Mary, and then having to put all those books back on the shelves (albeit in a haphazard fashion) because those had to go somewhere. Using my thighs for power—which was definitely waning by this point—I pushed my desk against that paneled wall, as well.

Alice was doing likewise with all of her student desks; she was dragging hers across her space over to my side where she and I together began hoisting each one up in order to stack on top of one of my student desks. With each hoist, Alice and I both had to emit loud groans just for the sheer energy to accomplish the task.

"Whoa, whoa, whoa! I can hear you two ladies even over this squeaky wheel. Hold on! Let me do that!" Beni arrived with his first heavy load of round tables, folded and stacked on a flatbed dolly. The second he saw what Alice and I were struggling to do, he took over, thank goodness, and finished heaping Alice's desks on top of mine so he could fit more tables in the open space. We both tried to help him, but he ordered us to take a breather. Once he had finished, Alice and I gawked at the precariously-built pyramid of desks as Beni then began unloading and setting up his first trip of round tables.

Karen moseyed into the room to check our progress. "Wow, it looks so big in here with everything cleared out of the way, doesn't it? Beni, I see you're bringing over the round tables from the maintenance/storage shed." Glancing at the newly-erected pyramid, she said, "Elizabeth, don't forget to set up those gray dividers in front of all these stacked desks so we (*What's this 'we' business?*) can try and hide them from view, all right?" I gave her a thumbs up. (Alice told me later that it was all she could do to restrain herself from giving Karen another finger.) "I need it to look nice in here for our guest specialist." Karen then moseyed right back out the door.

I followed her out into our B-Hall and managed to catch her before she exited to the courtyard. "Karen! In case you haven't heard, those 'dividers' as you call them tend to fall over with the slightest whiff of breeze, and I mean on an almost daily basis. Listen, I've had students occasionally get slammed on their heads and backs by them. If anybody accidently touches one while getting out of a chair, for example, or if you turn on those ceiling-mounted fans while either the classroom door to B-Hall or those double metal doors to the outside are also open, those flats are likely going to fall over, I'm just warning you—and maybe fall on somebody."

"Well, we'll just have to make sure those dividers are steady and not place the round tables and chairs too close to them, now, won't we?" *There's that 'we' again.*

Karen exited to the courtyard and probably to her office or to leave campus. I had a flash of longing for the comfy driver's seat of my car as I was ready to leave campus.

Meanwhile, Alice said with a shrug when I came back into the room, "At least you tried to warn her; I heard."

Another hour passed—another hour closer to dusk—before Alice and I determined that we had done all we could to follow through with Karen's instructions, in addition to offering what help we could to Beni. Alice and I each thanked him, and then, as we dragged ourselves to our respective cars, we could only hope the administration knew what they were doing by holding Monday's 'special' in-service with the 'special' out-of-state guest speaker in the milieu of the old industrial tech room. She and I had a 'special' sense of foreboding.

Arriving at 7:30 a.m. on Monday morning, I went straight to Mala's room. "Hey, can I park myself in here until things start? Admin has taken over my room."

"Sure. Let me guess, those jerks did not send help?"

"Nope."

"I can't tell you how mad that makes me," said Mala.

Jack came in with the coffee. The Breakfast Club was called to order. What had become customary for Jack, Jeb, Mala, Linzey Faith (when she wasn't irritated at us), and I was that we would gather early morning for ten minutes of coffee and conversation. With her after-school and evening rehearsals, as well as tech work (not to mention getting ready for the next day's lesson plan activities), Alice understandably had difficulty sparing even ten minutes before the school day started. She joined us whenever she could. Additionally, Dex generally didn't attend. Between grading all his English papers and helping Alice design and build Theatre sets did not allow time for socializing. Besides, wherever Alice was, there Dex would be, also. For those of us who consistently met, though, the camaraderie helped us ease the stress of teaching.

However, Mr. James was not pleased with our little group. We knew this because of his frequent and negative allusions to any clique of teachers who, in his opinion, were probably congregating as complainers and grumblers and who, by their attitudes, then served to stir up controversy and generate complaints among the whole faculty. No doubt, Mr. James was really delivering a warning: Room 13, stop visiting. We didn't. What rebels we were.

This morning's Breakfast Club topic was the in-service about to begin in the industrial tech room. Mala started with a wager. "Ten-to-one, a flat will fall over. One of you yahoos will start snickering—probably trying unsuccessfully to conceal it; then, the others of you will start chuckling; and then, good luck after that because you know I'm gonna bellow out a rooster of a cackle."

"Just as long as they keep the door shut, the current

from the ceiling-mounted industrial fans will not be as strong," I said.

Our reverie was interrupted when Francine's high heels tapped their way to Room 13's door. "Folks, sorry to break up your little session, but it's time to head to our in-service meeting." Jack, I noticed out of my peripheral vision, gave her a whip-crack of a salute.

"That's our cue, gang." Jeb collected our coffee mugs to take to his biology room. There, he had a little sink where he would rinse them out for us.

Jeb caught up with us as we entered the industrial tech room. What jumped out first was that we noticed a seating chart displayed on a large easel—a seating chart as if we were students who needed to be managed (or separated). Pointing to the seating chart drawn with black magic marker on a piece of white poster board, Mala gave a quizzical look to Karen, who stood beside the easel. To answer Mala's non-verbal query, Karen said, "We just believe that mixing subject areas makes for better on-task, collaborative discussions." The Breakfast Club was dubious. The goal was to separate us.

Francine, our high school principal's secretary, introduced Karen, our district curriculum specialist, who then introduced Dr. Bobbie Jensen, our district superintendent, who then introduced the guest curriculum specialist consultant, Margaret from Maine. She outlined the day's agenda with great expectations. Margaret then began the morning session.

Barely having gotten started, Margaret paused to ask, "Can you all hear me?"

"No!" a few teachers in the back shouted. "Can we turn off those fans?"

Karen traversed the entire room to our class door where the wall switches were located. The large, noisy fans hummed and whined to a dull stop. *Without fans, this room with all these faculty members in here is going to get hot.*

Meanwhile, Margaret broke from the seating chart arrangement and asked us to sit with our own curricular groups—probably again to the consternation of the district curriculum specialist and the assistant principal and the principal who all exchanged a furtive glance with each other, almost managing to hide their displeasure.

Mala and I were excited because now we could sit together. Alice, being the only theatre teacher in the district, sat with us. Jack and Jeb were at the science table next to us. With their proximity, we were like our Room 13 selves.

Our first small-group task was to choose verbs from Bloom's Taxonomy (a classification chart of cognitive skills) and apply them to our written objectives for the purpose of establishing higher-order thinking skills. "I have a verb for you—'waste'—as in we waste our time at in-service," said Jack.

"You know that we are research dummies for someone's PhD, don't ya?" said Jeb.

"Here, let me see the ridiculous list," said Mala as she snatched it out of my hands and popped the handout in the air a few times crisply. I was glad to have my friend back in a jovial mood. "Swan, you and I have already done this with our assignment templates."

"I know—but remember that Karen and Francine don't like our format? Go figure."

Perusing the list, we began underlining verbs that we had already incorporated into our interactive units. Although this activity was wasting our time, we cooperated and faked enlightenment.

Suddenly, someone from the Language Arts group projected across the room. "Can we please have those fans on again? This room is getting hot!" More voices from their table chimed in with agreement, one of those I recognized as Dex's. I noticed Alice's ears perked up at the sound of his voice, too.

Karen traversed the entire room once more to where the wall switches were located. She flipped the switches. The large, noisy fans hummed and whined again, this time to a dull start. Mr. James, being his helpful self, used a key on his master key ring to unlatch the padlock; unwind the thick chain from the two long handles; and then shove open each side of the double metal doors. With his foot, he dropped down the two door stops. Alice and I gave each other a knowing look of *uh-oh* and read the other's thought of *they better watch out for the falling flats!*

Mala put a voice to Alice's and my thoughts. "Oh, it's getting ready to hit the fan!"

Margaret from Maine, who had been circulating around the room and commenting on each group's progress, stopped at the math table which was right in front of a gray flat. Noticing an empty chair, she collegially invited herself to join that group for a moment.

Suddenly, the industrial-sized and ceiling mounted fans sucked in a strong gust of spring wind. Sure enough, two of the hinged and double-sided flats fell with a loud whack—one falling on the math group's table and the other, unfortunately, landing hard on Miss Margaret's head. The math teachers shrieked and jumped out of their chairs, some of which toppled over backwards or sideways onto the concrete floor. The only one from that table who didn't jump up was our out-of-state guest curriculum specialist. She was hunched over the table top, crying out in painful groans, holding the back of her head with both hands. Oozing blood appeared between her fingers.

Immediately, Francine, Karen, and Dr. Jensen hollered their shocked exclamations as they rushed to Margaret's side. They tried to help Margaret stand, but her knees buckled underneath her. As they supported her, she insisted that she needed to lie down. They helped her to that cold, concrete floor.

One of the science teachers from Jeb's and Jack's table obviously had rushed to get Mary from her nurse's station because they both came flying into the room pushing a wheelchair over to Margaret. Nurse Mary squatted down and bent over her patient, who was lying on her side. Mary pulled a pair of surgical gloves from her pocket to inspect the bleeding wound. I heard her say, "Oh, that's quite a gash you have. I'm thinking that a corner of the flat, where two pieces of wood come together in a sharp point, is what did this to you." After allowing Margaret to calm down somewhat and rest on her side for a few minutes—during which, by the way, one could have heard a pin drop—she then instructed the three administrators to help Margaret up from the floor and, after Mary had locked the brakes, they all helped settle her into the wheelchair. Mary positioned Margaret's feet on the foot supports and off they went with the three administrators tagging behind. As he exited, Mr. James instructed us faculty to remain seated until further notice.

Jeb leaned way over toward Alice and me. "Do they come running to help you guys when the flats fall?"

"Not so far," I whispered.

"What idiots thought, after we've told them, that the flats might not fall? Did they think we've been making this up, Elizabeth?"

"I guess so, Alice."

Jack chimed in with two more cents of his agitated opinions. "You know, that lady could sue the district, don't ya? Think about the potential publicity fallout from this little incident today. Headlines: 'Out-of-State Guest Consultant Educator Suffers Nasty Head Wound from School District Negligence—Invited Educator Expert Knocked Unconscious Due To Irresponsible School District—School District's Falling Flats Leave Guest Speaker Flat on the Floor, Head Gashed and Bloody."

I was never so glad to see Linzey Faith. She was like Paul Revere riding through our midst to deliver the scoop about this most recent ordeal. Making a bee-line for the two adjacent tables where us Breakfast Club colleagues sat, still sunk in disbelief, she announced the following. "I heard what just happened! Admin's and Mary were talking about it as they careened her in a wheelchair past my library door on the way to Dr. Jensen's office!"

"Wait, on the way to Dr. Jensen's office? Why? Why not the nurse's station so she could lie down?"

"Because, Elizabeth, Dr. Jensen's office has a lovely soft-suede heather-gray sofa. Don't you agree that the lady will be so much more comfortable lying down on that instead of Nurse Mary's metal gurney bed? And besides, taking her to Dr. Jensen's office makes a much nicer impression, wouldn't you agree?"

Sigh. "Yes, I do agree, Linzey Faith. That is at least something that does make sense. What else did you learn about how our guest specialist is doing? Anything?"

"Oh, yes. I was kind of secretly following them on my way back to the library. Good thing I have on soft-soled shoes today. Our Dr. Jensen told Francine and Mr. James that she is extremely concerned about liability and a law suit being filed against the school district!

She tore Mr. James a new one, chastising him for not thinking in advance about the potential danger of using your drama flats, Alice."

"Good grief! The superintendent was in our room last week. Alice and I had fully apprised her of the fact that those flats topple over onto students and desks and the floor, almost on a daily basis. Talk about throwing him under the bus! She's covering 'hers,' if you know what I mean," I said.

"Sounds like the case," said Linzey Faith. "She also ordered him to research the cost of remodeling the industrial tech room, but before you and Alice get too excited, Dr. Jensen said she wanted it to become an all-purpose event room for school board meetings, in-service meetings like you all had today—"

"The hell it better not be like the one we had today," Jack interrupted.

"—and community events."

"What, pray tell, are they planning to do with Alice and me?"

"I am sorry but that information I do not know. If a teacher resigns you could inherit that room or you could be traveling teachers next year." After I picked my jaw up off the cold-gray concrete floor, Linzey tossed in one more zinger. "Oh, another thing—the ambulance came."

"Ambulance?" Mala and I queried simultaneously.

"Yes," Linzey Faith stated matter-of-factly. "They're taking your guest speaker to the emergency room. I heard the paramedics tell her that she needed stitches."

"Stitches?" Again, Mala and I exclaimed the same word at the same time. This was getting to be a pattern.

"Stitches?" Alice echoed. "That is serious, y'all. I'm going to discuss this tomorrow with Mr. James. I'm gonna get up on my soap box again. This school district has been 'green clover-leaf-lucky' that one of our students, Elizabeth, has not yet been seriously injured. I mean, really. Just picture that on the six o'clock news, will ya, Jack?"

A student aide appeared in the doorway holding a folded piece of white paper and seemed to be searching for somebody. I was concerned when the somebody turned out to be me. I immediately recognized the note paper and Mr. James initials at the top right-hand corner. I opened and read what I was handed. The typed memo conveyed this message:

Elizabeth and Alice, please make sure that the gray drama flats do not fall on and injure a student. Student safety is very important. This will now require you both to think about the activities that you design for your classes. Thank you for your cooperation.

J. James.

After reading the memo once more, aloud to my Breakfast Club colleagues and especially since it was also addressed to Alice, I slammed it down on the table. "I appreciate and love you, Mala, but I cannot—do—this—anymore. Stick a fork in me, I'm done. It's all I can do to walk into this warehouse of a classroom one more day to finish out the last two months of this year, much less continue to try and teach in here another year. For Mr. John James to assume that we haven't put any thought into our activities—really? Speaking only for myself, I cannot do—will not do—traditional teaching anymore. That's not working with both Alice and me trying to teach in here, and it's certainly not going to work with me having to be a floating teacher next year or the coming years—if I even choose to stay here one more year. It has just not been effective, including for Alice's and my students." *Just shoot me now if we can't turn this around.*

Mala grasped my arm and encouraged me to sit back

down after I had bolted out of my seat in anger. Ever the voice of reason, she said, "All right, let's throw away the book and start over. We've got this! How 'bout it, gang? Breakfast Club, are you in for some creative, cross-curricular and multi-discipline lesson planning sessions? If so, let me see a pile-on of stacked hands here in the center of my table. Jeb and Jack, get your butts over here." Linzey Faith stepped back, unsure if she were to be included. "Get over here, Linzey Faith. You're going to be in on this, too." Smiling, Linzey Faith placed her hand on top of all of ours.

Tomorrow, by necessity, must not be another zoo-madhouse day like today. After all, necessity is the mother of invention.

EIGHT

Salsa Lessons

Arriving at school Tuesday morning, I was a mixed bag of fatigue and stress. Admittedly, however, I also held hope in my hands. My colleague friends and I had made a pact at the end of yesterday's in-service chaos, signified by our stacking of hands in a show of unity—the unity of a determined purpose to find solutions for my nearly impossible teaching circumstances.

On the heels of that chaotic in-service meeting the day before, not to mention the prior seven months having been no less chaotic from being made to share classroom space with drama, the clinic, and the falling flats, I was feeling almost defeated, almost ready to quit in one more month at the end of my first year in this school district.

I knew things had to change, so I headed straight for Mr. James' office. I pleaded with him to change my room for the next year. The only choices he could give me were either to be a traveling teacher next year or to continue, as is, in the old industrial tech room, still sharing it with Alice and her drama classes. He gave me these crumbs, though—he assured me that the tech equipment would be moved out over the summer and that the new clinic would be finished as well, so (trying to encourage me), he said things should be a little better. While I appreciated the crumbs, I did not share his enthusiasm.

Next, of course, I went to Room 13. There was my circle of hope: Mala, Jack, Jeb, Linzey Faith (and Alice, whom I knew, from the group pact of the previous afternoon, was a Breakfast Club partner in absentia this morning). I took a seat in a student desk, sighed, and propped my head in my hand.

"Uh-oh, I don't like the look of those dark circles under your eyes. Are you sick?" Mala asked.

"I can't do this anymore—not another year like this one. Mr. James just told me that I'd have to choose to be either a floating teacher next year, or to share the industrial tech room again with Alice and her drama kids. I told him things had to change—intimating that I might quit and not come back next year if they don't—but other than promising to move out that dusty old equipment and moving the nurse's clinic to its new location next year, that's all he could offer me, just those crumbs."

"Did I hear 'crumbs'?" Jeb entered carrying a vintage tray with the group's coffees but with the added enhancement of donuts. "I've got some crumbs for y'all—donut holes!" Noticing my demeanor, he said, "Hey, you don't look so good."

"It's all I can do, Jeb, to walk into that room one more time this morning. This has not been a year of good teaching experiences." Jack walked in and sat down. He quickly picked up on the mood and looked at Mala for a hint. She made the 'silence sign' with her finger. "I'm frustrated; my students are frustrated. I have got to think outside the box and throw away any kind of lecture or traditional approach."

"Well, that's why we made the group pact yesterday afternoon, isn't it? To come up with solutions?" Jeb handed out our respective mugs and placed the donut holes within easy reach of everyone.

After one sip of her coffee and chunking down a donut hole, Mala said, "The meeting of the Breakfast Club is now called to order. Gang, we need to put our heads together and help Swan. Put yourself in her shoes—no supplies, no ability to communicate effectively. What do you do to do better than just survive? What do you do to have you and your students thrive? Now, go! You have five minutes to think. Who has an idea—and fast, before she resigns! And by the way, dear colleagues, if she does, you won't want to be around me for the last month of this school year. Now—Jack and Jeb, you know what to do—hang 'em on the wall, and let's get to it. Let's brainstorm."

I actually offered up the first idea (something I had been pondering for quite some time). "Honestly, I think maybe a fun, student-centered activity would work best. That way, I could circulate among the various small groups and work with each one of those instead of trying to attempt whole group instruction over all the noise." I sipped my coffee, waiting for someone's response or another idea.

The group was deep in thought for a moment, allowing the caffeine to begin its work. Then, Jack said, "So what vocabulary are you working with currently?"

"Foods."

"Well, that's easy," Linzey Faith said. "The only fun thing to do with food is eat it." Her statement 'rang the bell,' so to speak.

Mala said, "That's it! You've hit upon something, Linz. Let me piggyback onto your idea—cooking! Why couldn't your students prepare a recipe in groups, Swan?"

"Like a cooking show, maybe, right?" said Jeb. "You could make it a competition."

"And we would get to eat the recipe from the winners, right?" added Jack as he snagged several donut holes for himself and popped them one-after-the-other into his mouth.

"Cooking…hmmm… I like it, but I don't have a foods lab, of course. Such an activity would have to be simple, such as 'shake and pour' or 'stir and eat,' right?"

"I've got it—salsa!" Mala beamed as she pronounced this resultant idea.

There it was. From a collaborative, multi-curricular group of misfit colleagues came a wonderful idea. Room 13 had already been my think tank and support group thus far this first year, but now, it would be even more so.

We quickly and roughly outlined the salsa lesson-plan activity. My compadres agreed to donate their blenders from home (as long as they got to eat some of the salsa, Jack reminded us). Mala and I made a simple and basic ingredient list for the students to bring: onion, tomatoes, and serrano peppers (all pre-chopped at home so they could wash their hands of sticky or fiery juices) and salt and pepper. We also included some optional ingredients to our list: garlic, jalapeno peppers, mangoes, pineapple, cumin; cilantro leaves; sugar; lime juice—just to name some (and, again, to be prepared at home where students had their water source). Finally, Mala and I drafted a quick list of Total Physical Response (TPR) warm-up activities for a cooking (or rather, a blending) activity. The Breakfast Club members agreed to meet after school and finalize all the details. I was energized and excited to try this new approach; Mala was relieved that I was no longer harboring the idea of resigning.

Wednesday, after organizing my Spanish students into groups of four, I handed each team a half-sheet of paper with the salsa recipe on it. Each group had to discuss the recipe and its basic—plus optional—ingredients; decide upon the ingredients they wanted to use; and determine who among them would bring which of the prepared ingredients. Additionally, each group had to work together to create their demonstration script, en español, as to how they chose to make their salsa; they had to assign speaking parts for each group member to say to the remainder of their observing class members.

I circulated among the small groups, helping each with essential vocabulary and phrasing. After ten more minutes, I would pause beside each group to listen to them rehearse their presentations and to give a critique with both positive feedback, as well as suggestions for improvement. I then asked them to develop the scoring rubric with expectations that they thought I should consider for grading each demonstration. (To differentiate, though, between the scoring rubric for my Spanish I versus my Spanish II students, I required my advanced-level students to develop a more challenging rubric for their demo talks.) Working with small groups was much easier than trying to teach to the whole class. The students were so excited and couldn't wait to perform the next day—not to mention, sample their culinary accomplishments.

The Breakfast Club, as promised, brought their blenders from home and met me on my side of the room before first period. "So, this is where all the magic's going to happen today, huh?" Jack said as he winked and handed me his blender.

"Hey, hand it over!" Mala and Linzey Faith were already arranging desks, four to a group, with one blender for each.

"Yep, I can only hope some magic happens in here today!" I answered as Jeb started pouring coffee into our respective mugs; he was our faithful barista.

"Those fans, alone, are loud enough. I can see how the noise just even from those would get to you, Liz. By the way, where's Alice?" Jack asked.

"Wherever Dex is, Alice is. They're probably on the stage designing the world's next greatest set," said Jeb.

"You know her rehearsals and tech work begin when the final bell rings, Jeb. She always says that's when her real job actually begins. She and her play production students are still up here at night when most of us have already had dinner, done our dishes, are bathing kid-dos and putting them to bed, and are probably grading papers while our favorite TV show is playing in the background. Alice usually rolls in right before the first-period bell."

Like clockwork, Alice walked through our classroom door, set her tote bag on top of her desk, and sure enough, the first-period bell rang. "I've obviously missed another meeting of the Breakfast Club. Y'all are in here this morning instead of Room 13?"

"Yep. Gotta keep admin guessing," I answered. "Hey guys, thanks for all the help. I'll touch base with you at lunch in Mala's room."

Drama and Spanish students began arriving. Mine quickly got into their groups. As soon as I had checked the roll, we practiced with TPR (a 'watch-listen-repeat-do' teaching and learning strategy). After a few minutes of practice, we were ready to begin our salsa lesson, ready to 'cook.'

Group I began as the other three groups observed and waited their turns. Group I demonstrated and orally explained in Spanish their selection, chopping, adding, and blending of their chosen ingredients. One benefit of a cinder block room with concrete floors is indestructibility, so making a mess was of no concern; however, any noise is amplified. The noise of the ceiling-mounted big and boxy industrial fans was amplified. The additional noise made by the blender was amplified. True, too, was the fact that just maybe I was talking extra loudly over the boisterously whirring blender. I'll admit to that.

Theatre Arts II, on the other hand, were rehearsing their duet scenes, which Alice always videotaped to support the critiques that she and students would give to each duet team prior to performances for a final grade. A disgruntled, hands-on-hips Alice Simmons suddenly appeared on my side of the room and yelled above all the other lovely noise, "What in sam-hill tarnation are y'all doing?"

"Making salsa," I hollered back over the heads of my students. "Want some?"

"Want some! Mrs. Jones, I am trying to record my students as they rehearse their scenes. I cannot have grinding blenders in the background. Are you nuts?"

"Well, since I've been trying to teach in this room all year— yes, I am most definitely nuts. What do you propose?"

Alice's exasperated look and roll of her eyes told me to allow her pause to think a moment.

"Okay, how many salsa groups do you have?"

"This period, I have four. How many minutes are your students' duet scenes?"

"Three-minute time limit. Why don't we each say to the other, '1-2-3-go'—or something like that?"

"All right, I could say loudly, 'uno-dos-tres'—and that could signal one of my student groups to run their blender, as well as it would signal you and the duet team you're videoing to not begin yet while my kids are blending. When you hear the blender noise stop, you then could yell over to us, 'one-two-three'—and we'd know to pause our salsa lesson activity and be quiet for a few minutes. Would that work for you, Ms. Simmons?"

"Yes, for now, I guess this plan will have to do. In the future, though, we really will need to coordinate better."

Ay caramba, No kidding. "Well, then, Ms. Simmons," I said sweetly and ever-so-politely, "may I suggest that tomorrow after school, before you get your rehearsal and tech activities cranked up, you come to Mrs. Smith's room and just touch base with her and me as to what our foreign language lesson plans are for the next school day. We could discuss what our various and especially noisy classroom activities are going to be so that maybe those would not compete with each other and might even complement and coordinate with each other?"

"All right. At this point in the year, I could sure use a brief break from my theatre world. I'll be there tomorrow afternoon, at least for a few minutes." The remainder of the day, back and forth we went: 'Uno-dos-tres, blend! One-two-three, scene!'

Also getting exasperated with this cacophony was Nurse Mary. At one point that morning, she had projected her voice through the thin, paneled wall asking if my Spanish students would be running blenders all day. When I answered 'yes,' she informed me that she had scheduled calling students into the clinic to review with them their immunization requirements. She told me later when we passed each other in a hallway that she had decided to wait a day to do all of that instead of trying to fit those conferences into the 'uno-dos-tres/ one-two-three' routine that Alice and I had cooked up.

The students loved the salsa lesson activity, and because of that, so did I. In fact, my collaborative and cross-curricular Breakfast Club colleagues and I gleaned several valuable, creative insights from that one activity. The outgrowth from these "salsa lessons" was that Mala and I began developing more interactive units that would work well for small-group, student-led, and teacher-facilitated instruction. Our new strategy was to create real-life situations that would drive the language skills needed to function in that particular situation.

NINE

Rock the Boat

Starting the next school year (my second with this district), I was asked to be a floating teacher. I had no classroom to call my own but instead floated to other teachers' classrooms every single bloomin' class period.

Mala and I decided to combine our classes and team teach two days a week, on Tuesdays and Fridays; we began implementing this immediately. Even though she and I mostly taught different levels of Spanish, we believed that our students would love the combination of skills and activities—and they did. This approach made it easier to design lesson plan objectives and activities. Depending on the activity, we would alternately either hold class in Room 13 (whenever Mala wanted to stay put in her room); the cafeteria (whenever lunch was not in session); the library (whenever Linzey Faith granted her approval); or outside in the courtyard (whenever weather permitted). In order to accommodate the different levels of learners, we differentiated the skills and expectations so as to engage all of our students.

The administration, on the other hand, was not excited by Mala and me team teaching, and they were especially not pleased about us switching locations those two days out of every week. Our admins got quite aggravated trying to find us for their various and sundry reasons.

Moreover, our high school admins informed Mala and me that they were receiving noise complaints about our combined classes (which met here, there, and yon). When Mala and I informally surveyed our colleagues, however, we discovered only one complainer—Sandra the calculus teacher. Her room was one of those right next door to the cafeteria; Mala and I made sure from then on to have our combo class meet toward the opposite end of the café from Sandra's room.

If it wasn't the 'where are you' issue or the 'noise disturbance' issue, then the other category of complaint about us had to do with the 'essential elements' issue. Texas had instituted what was termed the "Essential Elements" as educational standards to which every lesson plan activity had to correspond. The admins continually questioned whether Mala's and my teaching strategies and techniques aligned with those EEs. When the state's new TEKS system (short for Texas Essential Knowledge and Skills) was implemented that replaced the Essential Elements, our admins again would ask for validation that our lesson plan activities, especially our team-taught ones, correlated to each requirement listed in the TEKS for foreign language. As Mala and I certainly knew, our communicative and real-life applications approach was actually fully supported by the TEKS—*as if Mr. James really understood our new state standards and mandates, anyway!* More than obvious to both Mala and me was that neither our high school nor our upper-level administrators were ever going to understand our philosophy for foreign language teaching and learning.

Now that we were team-teaching and developing authentic situations for our students, though, we believed our learning strategies that we designed for our Spanish students should be performance-based. We understood, of course, that students remember a foreign language much better when they have to use it (to paraphrase the old adage—if you don't use it, you'll lose it).

In our endeavors to create performance-based, real-world learning activities, Alice became a great resource for us. For example, she gave Mala and me the idea to do a children's theatre outreach to the second and third-grade elementary students in our small district.

We both would divide each of our own Spanish students into ensemble groups—netting about four to five ensembles for my students and about the same for Mala's. Generally, each small group was comprised of approximately four to five students. The groups were asked to create in written form a script. I allowed my Spanish I students to create theirs in English first, and then translate and transcribe into Spanish with my help, as needed. Mala's and my advanced students, on the other hand, were encouraged to try and think and write in Spanish from the 'get-go.' Each ensemble would then assign roles and rehearse their skits. At some point during the rehearsal phase, each ensemble team of a class period was required to present their skit to a small team from Alice's drama class. Her students would then give Mala's and my Spanish students both written and oral critiques to help improve their presentations. Each of these phases of development earned our students daily grades. The exciting culminating activity for my Spanish students, which earned them a more major grade, was for each ensemble to perform for one classroom of either second or third-graders at the elementary campus.

Collaboratively speaking, the Spanish students learned

how to improve communication and presentation techniques; Alice's drama students, in addition to developing their directorial skills, also learned some Spanish phrases (always helpful when living in Texas). Out of a noisy salsa activity that had occurred one day near the end of my first year there came this 'cool' cross-curricular activity. Regarding foreign language teaching strategies and techniques around the state, if not the nation, Mala and I had landed on something radically new for foreign language departments. For us now, gone were the days of teacher-directed learning, textbook lessons, only, with their grammar and reading comprehension exercises. Gone were the miniscule dialogues for student dyad groups to memorize and present for a grade. Finally, gone are the language lab activities with its earphones spilling out phrases in the foreign language that each individual student would then pronounce back into the speaker system connected to the teacher's listening ears. Mala and I were rebels—but not without a cause!

We knew that a little bit of fun goes a long way (with students of any age). When Jeb's biology students were studying endangered species, Mala's and my students studied endangered species in Spanish. The same topic studied in two different classes reinforced our students' knowledge. Sometimes, these activities would require short dialogues; writing, directing, and acting in a skit;

or producing a product, such as a video. All activities had scoring rubrics, to which our students contributed input, for both written language responses and presentational language responses.

Additionally, this second year, Mala and I inherited the middle school foreign language program. The state had not adopted a textbook for these exploratory/introduction to language courses; therefore, Mala and I created twelve vocabulary units, each with multiple activities. In order for our students to interact with these units more productively, we designed an elementary outreach program so that our middle school students could teach the vocabulary units to the elementary children. Showing off for the elementary classes was exciting for middle schoolers and increased their confidence-level in using Spanish. Thus, as educators, Mala and I were challenged to require more from our students than the memorizing of vocabulary, but now to apply the vocabulary to a real-life situation.

One afternoon Mala and I were brainstorming interactive activities for our students. South Texas had a Latino culture that played into our curriculum perfectly. "You know—" Mala said, but then paused as she pondered before speaking again. "What about a market type of activity? The students could make some kind of product—arts and crafts or food—representative of the

Latino culture, and then using their Spanish-language skills, they would engage in bargaining with their class-mates to try and sell their product. We could survey our students and have each brainstorm his or her own ideas as to what each student's product might be."

"Is money going to be a problem for some of our low-er-income students to purchase whatever supplies or ingredients they need in order to create their project?"

"For those in need who speak to us privately, we could help from our foreign language budget; we could surely purchase some, if not all, of their necessary items."

"Do you see my class bargaining with your class?" I said.

Suddenly her eyes widened with excitement. "Light bulb! A light bulb just came on in my brain. Let's really shake things up. Are you ready?"

"Uh, maybe. Mala, what are you thinking?"

"Let's invite the whole school!" Mala outlined her idea. "We will start by explaining the mercado/market con-cept to our students. I have a video we can use to start the discussion. Next, Swan, let's bring in any of our souvenirs that we've each brought back from our own vacations in Mexico. I think that showing them those will help them to brainstorm for their own product to sell. We could establish Fridays as our culture day, don't you think? First, we'll give our students time, of course, to develop their ideas. They'll be divided into small groups, with each group being its own 'company.' We will introduce new vocabulary for bargaining and selling and buying, plus we'll need to review numbers for the different currency values. We, as teacher-facilitators, can circulate around to all of our small groups, allowing them each to role-play with us until they are comfortable with the language necessary for this mercado unit."

"Oh, I like it." This idea really lit a fire under me, too.

"Monopoly money could work for currency while we role play."

"Mala! What about this? When the student body comes to our students' Spanish mercado—which we could set up in the courtyard, by the way—they would need to stop at the customs booth that some of our students would man; they'd need to get their passports stamped. Next, they'd have to go to our money-exchange booth where some of our students would be in charge of exchanging their real American currency for our pesos falsos that you and I could make, along with the help of some of our more artistic students."

"¡Fantástico! I love those ideas! Beni can bring tables out to the courtyard for us, and our students can decorate them like market booths. In fact, there's a whole 'nother class activity for them—to study typical designs for a Mexican mercado and then create those to have ready for decorating early that morning before first period—"

"—or after school the day before the mercado project," I inserted.

"Right. Good. Ha! Just had a thought: Can't we just see Little Miss No-Noise Sandra letting her calculus classes out to come to our mercado?"

"Oh-ho, no. Money math won't cut it. That's too low-brow for her intellectual proclivities. Hey, another concern—what if we develop a percentage, similar to tax brackets, for each student company to use for booth rental. You know some groups will sell more than others."

"Good thinking, Swan."

"Our students, after they determine their profit and pay off-the-top amount for 'rental' of their booth space, could convert their pesos falsos back into American currency. Each small-group 'company' could then receive back from us a portion of their profit, based on the percentage table we create, to be divided equally among their company members. Higher earning companies will pay more for booth space than companies with smaller profits to be fair to our special populations that participate. This will require companies to keep records in order to get their profit."

"Yah, we are brilliant, if I do say so myself. Earning some real money is going to be real motivation for our students! We deserve a pat on the back, Swan! Now, however, we must sell this entire idea to Mr. James. Are you up for that challenge?"

"Sure. We gotta do what we gotta do" (and we did do what we had to do; we made a presentation to our principal). A week passed before we heard back from Mr. James.

Entering Room 13, he said to Mala and me, "Ladies, we have a problem."

"Really, what is it?" I asked.

"Well, I don't think your market unit is going to work."

"Really? And why not?" Mala asked.

"It doesn't support the curriculum and student safety is a concern. The superintendent and I were talking and we think that you two should—"

"Hold it," Mala interrupted, "you were reading the standards for foreign language?"

"Now, Jean, don't start with me."

"Okay, wait a minute," I said. "How about let's start with me, then? I've got some things to say. Jean and I have spent a month preparing this unit—and that was in addition to the regular vocabulary and grammar instruction. This unit will give our students a real-world, authentic way to connect with and communicate in the language. First, for this unit, we have integrated marketing and economics concepts. Second, we have taught the history of the mercado or market concept in Latin America. Third, we have shown our students authentic products in order to inspire them to design and create their own; how to bargain according to Spanish merchant/cultural customs; and have worked with them regarding money conversion and exchange rates."

"That may all be well and good, but—"

"Moreover, Mr. James, we are giving the entire student body and faculty the opportunity to experience this exciting foreign language enrichment opportunity. Even if you look at the EEs or the proposed list of new standards—which are "Communicate, Connect, Compare, Culture, and Community—those five C's are all covered. So now, exactly which standards and elements of the foreign language curriculum give you and the superintendent concern that our mercado unit of study falls short, Mr. James?"

He didn't have an answer but stood, staring. "I didn't come to argue about this," he meekly mumbled.

"Perhaps, let's just call this what it is, shall we? The superintendent and you think that Elizabeth and I are rockin' the boat, right? You two are uncomfortable with the student body being out of class and with our non-traditional teaching and learning methods that she and I are now using. What's the real concern here? I mean, we teachers understand that you are under the thumb's pressure from Superintendent Jensen; she is under the thumb's pressure from the school board; and they, in turn, are under pressure from parents and the community and the Texas Education Agency. The pressure for excellent, standardized test scores trickles down, all the way to us teachers and our students. I assure you, Mr. James, that the curricular study units that Elizabeth and I develop either meet and/or exceed the state's mandated Essential Elements and this district's curriculum mandates. Our foreign language students are well-served.'

"Well, speaking of the students—yes, we are concerned for them, and yes, this isn't a traditional approach—especially with your outdoor market. It's going to have so many kids outside of their classrooms. Who will monitor all those students?"

"You," Mala pointed right at him, "as well as the teachers who will escort their own students to the courtyard for the mercado experience."

I spoke up again. "Mr. James, I tried to use a traditional approach last year—my first year here. Making that difficult, however, were these facts. I had to share a classroom with drama classes on one side of me and the nurse's station through a thin-paneled wall on the other side of me. Trying to lecture and engage with my students while contending with those noisy, industrial, ceiling-mounted fans—in addition to the understandable noises of drama classes and the occasional disturbing noises and unpleasant smells that sometimes emanated from the nurse's office—were all but impossible. I did not have a chalk board or a dry erase board. I did not have an overhead projector so that I could use transparencies to project lessons onto some bare wall. Heck, I didn't even have a wall; old, dusty equipment lined up along the only possible wall impeded that effort. Now, my second year here, I've been made to be a floating teacher. Circumstances are no better because I don't even have a classroom. From room to room to room and across the courtyard and then back across the courtyard, I'm having to push a heavy cart loaded with my textbooks, notebooks, workbooks, lesson plan book, students' papers, and office supplies, I don't have a chalkboard or dry erase board to call my own; I don't always have access to an overhead projector to use in the various rooms to which I float. You tell me—better yet, Mr. James—you come shadow me for one entire school day and show me how to do 'traditional' in my current situation; too bad I didn't think to ask you to do that last year."

"Okay, okay. I see your point, Elizabeth, but I am still concerned about all the noise from so many students being outside in the courtyard and moving around freely. That thought is unsettling."

"Show me a quiet, day-to-day foreign language class, and I'll show you students that aren't learning oral communication and conversational skills," Mala said. She continued. "Tell us what will make this work for you and Dr. Jensen? What do Elizabeth and I need to do in order to receive your approval, as well as Dr. Jensen's?"

"Write your proposal, documenting the new standards. Give that to me, and I will 'work on' the superintendent. Maybe see if you can get some of your parents to help supervise. Oh, and let me add this: Elizabeth, Francine and I are working on your room situation for next year. I promise."

"Thank you," I said. "I appreciate that, Mr. James."

Two weeks and two proposal attempts later, Mala and I finally were setting up the courtyard for our mercado event. Coordinating with the Cinco de Mayo celebrations in Texas, this was perfect timing, too.

All the Spanish classes had been field tripped to participate in the market during their Spanish class time and their lunch time. As soon as the bell for first period rang the first period Spanish students set up their booths. Fifteen minutes into the period the music began and the classes were allowed to come out and stroll through the Market. When they got to the bottom of the steps they had to pass through customs and then exchange their American currency into pesos falsos. The student venders only spoke Spanish and only accepted Mexican currency. It was our dream to immerse the students into a Spanish speaking culture as close to being in Mexico as possible.

The first period visitors were slow to engage but by second period the word was out. Come to the market! Our idea had worked and all student companies had earned some money. The parents got involved and donated time, materials, and their supervisory expertise. They were very supportive because their students loved our class. They were so excited to learn some Spanish and use it to shop for products from student vendors. At the end of the day we were exhausted but also proud at the excitement of the community. We received many compliments from our colleagues and tons of praise from the parents in the community.

The Breakfast Club had heard nothing but praise from the students and parents. It had been a battle to get the approval for our market project, but it had been a great success! My second year had ended on a positive note. Mala and I were now motivated to continue developing immersion situations.

Starting my third year there, I was given a classroom of my own. *Hallelujah!* Unfortunately, this room was in A-Hall, Room 2, still far away from Mala's in D-Hall. *Beggars can't be choosers, though, can we?*

As if we weren't busy enough with the start of a new school year, Mala and I decided to implement a portfolio system for student assessment. Embedded into our district-wide curriculum changes was the requirement to employ different forms of assessment: formative, summative, and alternative. Mala and I really liked the concept of portfolios because those were an alternative, summative assessment that offered a portrait of each student's learning.

The portfolio method of assessment had been around for some years, but mostly used by teachers working within the fine arts, performing arts, and language arts arenas—and only a few models from foreign language educators. The struggle for teachers assessing the learning progress of foreign language students had been with traditional numeric grades. A numeric grade could be quite misleading about any given child's ability to think in and then engage in oral communication skills using any particular foreign language. For years, we had heard people as adults say something like, "You know, I made an 'A' in my Spanish class, but I can't speak it." To hear such statements were so frustrating for us, as foreign language teachers.

A number does not fully provide a portrait of what a child knows—and I say that probably regarding and pertaining to any subject area. A picture, a portrait, paints a thousand words; thus, Mala and I created a foreign language portfolio system that was aimed to provide our students' parents with a more 'fleshed out' and detailed picture of their child's learning.

Knowing how questionably supportive the administration had been about our prior 'out-of-the-box' projects, Mala and I first pitched our portfolio idea to Mr. James. We asked him if we could reserve the cafeteria for the night of the soon-upcoming fall semester open house. We wanted that large space for our foreign language classes so that our students would have plenty of room and tables and chairs to be able to sit and share their learning with their parents. There, our visitors and students would get some refreshments (provided by us, of course); our students would then sit with their parents and peruse through their portfolios, explaining the various pieces of evidence that supported their learning achieved and learning-in-progress. Mr. James seemed more amenable than ever previously, but he said that he must, of course, get approval first from Dr. Jensen.

A few days later, he informed Mala and me that Dr. Jensen was concerned. Her concern was that we, as teachers, would not be the ones leading the discussions about our students' learning performance. In response, we further explained to Mr. James (for him to communicate directly to Dr. Jensen) that we certainly would be available, circulating throughout the cafeteria, to those in attendance to answer any questions or discuss any concerns that a parent might have. Mr. James put us 'on hold' again. He went back to our superintendent once more with our proposal and now with our answers to her concerns and objections. Later, after school that day, he called Mala and me to his office and informed us that Dr. Jensen was still not in great favor of our idea.

Mr. James, on the other hand, gave us his approval and

we almost fainted. Mala, skeptical, said, "Wow, are you feeling okay? Since when do you not follow Dr. Jensen's decisions? What's the catch?"

"Yes, I'm curious, too. What's the deal here? Are you retiring?" I asked.

"I thought you two would be happy. By the way, I also say 'yes' to you two reserving the cafeteria."

"We are happy. We are just surprised that you didn't ask for validation or research on portfolios. We must be getting better at providing you with information," I said, teasing him a little bit.

"Don't let this go to your heads because you two are pains to work with, but I do actually think that your foreign language program works."

I looked at Mala; she looked at me. We both were speechless—our mouths opened in surprise. "Oh my gosh. Did you just say that you think our immersion projects actually work?" I said.

"I can tell that the Spanish students really love to come to both of your classes. You don't see that often and your enrollment numbers are increasing."

"So, next year, can we actually have our classroom next

door to each other? That would make co-teaching and lesson plan coordination much easier," I said.

"Ladies, I am not that crazy."

"And...he's back to normal," Mala said. "C'mon, Swan. Let's go continue planning for our student-led portfolio conferences."

Three days later, the fall semester open house evening was awesome and exciting—for both us and, we observed, for our students and parents, too. The portfolio system became the starting point of communication with parents; even more ideal, this system was student-led. Our students showed their own portfolio to their parents and used it to help them explain what they've learned and were in the process of learning.

The cafeteria was filled with our Spanish students and their parents, grandparents, and siblings. As parents looked through their children's portfolios, we had them fill out a rubric that asked for what they saw as their child's areas of excellence, as well as areas that they believed needed improvement. Each student/parent team had to design a plan for success. (In the event that a parent could not attend this open house, an applicable student would share with us or with another teacher whom they admired and had brought to the cafeteria with them.)

Mr. James and our assistant principal Francine Davis were actually complimentary of our portfolio event. Especially gratifying was that the parents and family members of our Spanish students loved it. The positive feedback assured Mala and me that we were on the right track for successful foreign language instruction and learning.

Mala and I realized that we were on the right track with lesson plans involving real-world scenarios and real-life situations that necessitated full immersion of our students into the Spanish language and culture. Enter the Chihuahua Bats.

TEN

What is a Chihuahua Bat, Anyway?

The question begs to be asked, "What is a 'chihuahua bat,' anyway?" To answer that, I must recount Mala's and my first big adventure with our Spanish students. The answer stems from a border town hotel room; two passionate, lesson-agenda planners; and a wrinkled t-shirt stretched over the breadth and depth of a reclining, buxom librarian.

Once Mala and I began in earnest creating and implementing foreign language immersion activities using real-life situations, we knew the next step was to totally immerse our students in Spanish. Taking students 'in country' was the best way to accomplish that.

Over the winter break of my third year at North

Gate, and for the ensuing summers (when many other teachers were typically trying to decompress from the school year that just ended), Mala and I would organize language-immersion trips to Mexico for our students, our colleagues, and our own families. When the goal is to get a novice learner of a foreign language to actually use that new language, then drop them into a country where—when they get hungry enough—they will find the words they need. If they want to eat, they'll figure out the words to use!

Many of our first-time travelers were truly afraid to travel in Mexico. News media didn't help. TV channels and newspapers occasionally would do segments on some travel nightmare that had recently happened in Mexico, thus strengthening the fears of our prospective travelers. As a result, Mala and I developed what we called a 'first-step program' that would merely introduce our students to Mexico, much like first dipping a big toe in the water before diving in, so to speak.

We chose a weekend that spring of my third year to take a group across the Texas border into Nuevo Laredo, Mexico. There, we gently introduced them to the authentic Mexican culture. We stayed at a hotel on the United States side of the border. From it, we gave our students the 'big-toe-dipping experience' by walking our first-timers through customs and across the border just for the day, returning back to the U.S. side before sundown.

One fun activity that Mala and I concocted was a scavenger hunt whereby our students had to search for various locations—such as a doctor's office, a grocery store, a bank, a pharmacy, and a post office—that would require them to use a variety of Spanish vocabulary and phrases. The first group to find all of the places, checking those off their list and securing valid signatures of an employee and his/her position at each location, was the winner. Our winners' prize would be an item from the market—something garish, such as an over-sized and flamboyant sombrero—that we then hoped would evoke questions from the locals (hence, forcing the winners and their fellow-sojourner amigos to communicate with both listening and speaking skills in Spanish).

On one such "First Step Weekend" that same spring semester, we granted Linzey Faith her plea to join us. Linzey Faith loved to travel. Equally as much, she loved to research, so she was a helpful asset in researching and planning for the trip with us.

However, when learning that their overly-strict librarian, otherwise known as "Rigid Rules Reinerd," would be accompanying all of us, some of our students were less than enthusiastic. Another telling nickname some students had for her was "Book Nazi." In her defense, though, she had worked with teenagers for years; knew their sometimes wily and lackadaisical ways; and therefore, had to be strict about all the public's money that her library's books represented. Still, not a day would escape before we had heard a complaining comment about "Rigid Rules Reinerd" did this, or the "Book Nazi" did that.

Our Spanish students, no more angels than the rest of our student body, often came to Mala and me grumbling about the "this's" and the "that's." Another part of preparing youngsters for the real world, though, is to teach them that they are not the center of the universe; to acknowledge and accept that all kinds of people make the world go round; and to be open to having their perspectives changed by viewing people and places and situations (such as that of fearful expectations about traveling in Mexico) through a new lens, unfiltered by the wrinkles of preconceived notions and prejudicial bias.

Speaking of wrinkles...here's how the "chihuahua bat" term came into existence. As soon as we had arrived at our hotel in Laredo for the particular First Step Weekend in which Linzey Faith had traveled with us, we checked our students into their rooms, and then we three adults checked into ours.

Having barely just settled into our room (curtains drawn, lamp on), Mala and I sat with our cups of hotel room coffee at the small round table with our lesson planners laid out before us. Linzey Faith had kicked off her black flip flops adorned with oversized crystals and had claimed one of the king beds for herself. There she lay, pink-pedicured feet crossed at the ankles. Meanwhile, over at the table, Mala and I were cracking ourselves up with laughter while brainstorming, chattering, and devising some silly and fun activities for when we took our students on their first foray into a border town.

Suddenly, Linzey Faith (being single, living alone, and used to always having her own way without any interference) bolted upright in her bed. "Hey, pipe down, you two! I need a nap after that road trip, just maybe a twenty-minute power nap; otherwise, I may not can join in with whatever crazy schemes you two are cookin' up."

"Swan and I are planning the details of the scavenger hunt for our students. We'll try to be quieter, Linz," promised Mala. (*Are you kidding?* I thought. *Whenever we get together to plan, there is no such thing as quiet!* This situation was going to be a challenge, I knew.)

"I was just beginning to doze off, too, when one of you let out a loud cackle. I can't sleep now. Can you guys leave? Maybe go sit outside by the pool and do your crazy planning?"

Then, it happened. I could see the spiteful look in Mala's eyes, aimed like arrows at the reclining Miss Reinerd, but I knew that I could do nothing to redirect the conversation.

Mala stood up, marched over to the foot of the king-size bed upon which our school librarian reclined, and said, "Linzey Faith, who invited whom on this trip? Hmmm, oh, yes. We invited you—and now, you want to kick us out of our room in which you are our guest? Really? That's some gratitude."

"Look, girls, I just need a nap." With that, Linzey Faith lay back down, pulling her black sleep mask down over her eyes. "Twenty minutes, maybe?"

"Okay, fine," said Mala, as if talking to a woman in a black-out coma. "Swan and I will leave, but answer me this: What the hell does that say on your t-shirt? 'Chihuahua Bat'—what the hell is a 'chihuahua bat,' anyway? Some kind of hippie thing, I'm guessing!"

Linzey Faith kind of does look like a hippie today, I mused as I joined Mala at the foot of Linzey Faith's bed. *At the very least, a flower child, what with that long-fringed suede purse she brought embroidered with the 1960's peace sign.*

Hmmm, now noticing she's changed out of the traveling clothes she wore in the presence of our students into her frayed blue jean shorts and t-shirt (sans brassiere).

"What do you mean, 'chihuahua bat'—there's no such thing as a 'chihuahua bat'—how stupid is that? Everyone knows there's no such thing as a 'chihuahua bat.' My shirt says 'Chihuahua Bar.' I know you teach Spanish, but can't you read English?" *Whoa. This is not gonna be good,* I worried.

Linzey Faith petulantly pulled and stretched her shirt down and over and across her 'large personality'—or rather (ahem) her well-endowed 'hills and valleys'— and said sarcastically, "See. It says 'bar,' okay?"

Oh, yes, we can see all right. Lying down, Linzey Faith's t-shirt fabric followed the ups and downs, the ins and outs, of her relaxed form; thus, the formation of the lettering was somewhat distorted. Obviously.

Mala, taking a second look, blandly said, "Oh. Yes. 'Bar.' It says 'bar.' But it looked like it said 'bat.'

"Well, I can't imagine why it looked like 'bat' to you!" Mala and I looked at each other. We both knew why, but we didn't bother to explain it to Miss Hills and Valleys. I could see that Mala was trying to stifle a giggle, as was I.

"Must be my new bifocals. Can't see a thing with these." All it took was one more look from Mala to me, and the giggles broke through some failed 'stifle barrier.' We knew it was time to leave Linzey Faith and let her get her beauty sleep before we insulted her even more with our laughter. Besides, Mala's smiling mouth did not camouflage or distract me from her incensed eyes. She was boiling over Linzey Faith's 'stupid' comment and the 'can't you read English' comment. *Time to leave.* I hooked my arm through Mala's and hauled her out into the hotel hallway and down to the pool.

There, we resumed planning our scavenger hunt activity. A few of our students jumped out of the pool (only kids will swim in cold pool water in spring, right?) and padded over to us, dripping wet.

"Hey, Señoras! What are you two doing?"

"Hey, guys! Would you believe it—Mrs. Jones and I were kicked out of our own room by our guest-room-mate who complained that we were too loud for her to take a quick nap."

"No way, Señora Smith!" Several students exclaimed all at once, "Miss Rigid Rules, right?"

"Yep. She's trying to nap, and Mrs. Jones and I were trying to laugh. Nappin' and laughin' don't mix, I guess, so here we are—booted outside. Actually, we're planning some fun activities for you guys!"

"Like what?" they excitedly asked.

"That's a surprise. You'll find out soon enough. Hey, guys, let me ask you a question. Do you believe there is such a thing as a chihuahua bat?"

The dripping wet students exchanged looks and shrugs. One of them answered, "We dunno, but sure, if you say so, Señora."

"Okay, okay. Hmmm…be thinking about that concept, will y'all, and when we get back to school, I'm going to ask you all to draw what you think a chihuahua bat looks like. Deal?"

"Deal! But why?"

Mala kept it 'clean' by only explaining that their librarian's t-shirt was all wrinkly, making the wording on the front of her shirt appear to say "Chihuahua Bat" instead of something else, and that because Mala had mis-read it, the so-named Rigid Rules had gotten extremely agitated and kicked her two trip hosts out of their own hotel room. Our students were on our side, of course.

That pool-side discussion consequently launched

the great "Chihuahua Bat Campaign." Once back at school on Monday morning, following our "First Step Weekend" Laredo trip, we couldn't wait to tell the chihuahua bat story to our Breakfast Club colleagues who jumped right on that band wagon. Jack and Jeb didn't waste a minute before they launched their good-natured ribbing. Jack and Jeb lived to make fun of Mala and me. By mid-morning, first morning back, both Mala and I began to be greeted in the halls by fellow faculty as the "Chihuahua Bats"—a school grapevine operates quickly.

Meanwhile, Mala and I asked our respective Spanish students to provide us with their renderings of what they imagined would be the appearance of a so-called "chihuahua bat." For example, they provided us with "Flasher Bat" in a trench coat; "Baggin' & Saggin' Bat" in saggy jeans; "Rugrat Bat"; "Ren & Stempy Bats"; and "Mr. Spock Bat." Their renderings were quite unique and entertaining.

Of course, Jeb the Jokester (not to be outdone) did his own imaginatively-drawn concoctions of the mythical chihuahua bat—in the form of several satirical cartoons poking at Linzey Faith's sensitivities. He posted these, of course, on the faculty bulletin board in the workroom located within the library, Miss Rigid Rules Reinerd's library. Some of his captions read, "Beware: The

Chihuahua Bats are Coming to a Hallway (or Library) Near You!" or "See Nurse for Your Bat Shots Now! Get Vaccinated; Get Protected!" or as one final example, "Chihuahua Bats: Purveyors of Fun; Disrupters of Peace!"

Linzey Faith Reinerd, for her part in the drawn-out conflict that had originated in the Laredo hotel room, kept up with her seemingly continuous comment to any and all who'd lend her a sympathetic ear: "Everyone knows there is no such thing as a chihuahua bat! How stupid! Obviously, the Spanish-teaching Mrs. Smith and her straight-laced sidekick have difficulty reading plain English. My t-shirt said 'Bar,' just as plain as the back of my hand." Upon getting wind of that statement, I needed to keep Mala's temper in check. Mala figuratively wanted to give the back of her hand to our not-so-grateful travel buddy.

We had to fight back. Sneaking into the library one late afternoon, Mala and I took down and hid away Rigid Rules Reinerd's neat and tidy "Tips for Successful Reading" bulletin board. In other words, Mala and I used our artistic talents to redesign her six-foot long by four-foot deep central bulletin board by replacing her cut-out stencil lettering, her visual graphics, and her book covers representing some of the world's great literature with our Spanish students' colorful and fantastical drawings of chihuahua bats. We plastered her entire bulletin board, layer-upon-layer like a collage, with nothing but chihuahua bat images.

The next day—and we didn't even put them up to this—we began hearing from faculty and students that some of our Spanish students had been asking Ms. Reinerd all kinds of 'bat questions' for their allegedly-assigned research papers on the enigmatic topic. As she would assist them in locating books on bats, they said would exclaim, "Oh, no, Miss. We need books on chihuahua bats."

As reported by the grapevine to us, Miss Reinerd's exasperated and perturbed voice could be heard outside the walls of the library (located in Main Hall). The grapevine reported that she, in no uncertain terms, vociferously insisted to our students that there is no such thing as a chihuahua bat.

"Then why do you have them all over your bulletin board, Miss?"

During one such interaction with some of our Spanish students (who were only too glad to goad their so-called Rigid Librarian), Miss Reinerd could no more take this extended teasing. She slapped down onto a table all of the various resource books about bats that she had painstakingly pulled; she marched in a mighty huff over to her bulletin board; and she unceremoniously ripped down the students' drawings. After wadding them all up into one giant paper ball, she hauled it and herself out of the library and headed straight for us in Room 13. Our lunchtime gang were each just sitting down to enjoy our soups, sandwiches, and salads when in she stormed. Like a tornado, she blasted us.

"I do not appreciate people breaking into my library and messing with my bulletin board displays. My library is a place of respect!" She then angrily slam-dunked the giant paper chihuahua bat ball into Mala's trash can. The tornado stormed out as madly as it had stormed in. We were speechless in the ensuing aftermath of silence that follows such storms. For ten seconds we sat with our mouths gaping open as wide as our eyes.

Jeb broke the ice. "I'm pretty sure I saw fire come out of those nostrils of hers. You two are in trouble."

Mala's own nostrils flared. "Well, if she just hadn't kept being so nasty after we returned from our Laredo trip! This was all because of the wrinkled writing on her t-shirt. That's why the damn 'bar' word looked like the damn 'bat' word. And then, returning to school—yes, Swan and I told the tale of the hotel room pseudo-brawl to you guys; then our students picked up the gauntlet and ran with it; but then Linzey Faith had to keep on keepin' on makin' her snide and ignominious comments about what she perceived as my stupidity and illiteracy of the English language. I had no choice. I had to fight back. Miss Linzey Faith Reinerd has met her match in Swan and me."

"And, after all, you two are obviously now the 'Chihuahua Bats,' said Jeb the Satirical Cartoonist who had his own role in exacerbating the tensions.

"And Chihuahua Bats must defend their honor," said Jack.

"We'll give her some space, Mala, and pray she doesn't sabotage the school's only copier located in her library," I said.

Yes, we had 'crossed the line' with our fellow colleague-librarian. Mala, in her defense, didn't like being ridiculed, and me right along with her—especially since we had paid for and had graciously included her on our out-of-town excursion with our students.

Jack and Jeb humorously promulgated us as the 'Chihuahua Bats' around the school and, indeed, around the district—including to the administration. To the faculty, administration, and even to some among the student body, we were no longer solely Mrs. Smith and Mrs. Jones; to our inner circle Breakfast Club clique, we were no longer merely Jean and Elizabeth; heck, even to ourselves, we were no longer just Mala and Swan; to just about everyone on the North Gate campus, extending to our district's several other schools, we became known as the 'Chihuahua Bats.'

The admins, faculty, and staff began to operate with something akin to that 1984 movie's mantra, 'Who Ya Gonna Call?'—the Chihuahua Bats!—whenever some sticky-wicket 'problem project' needed a couple of problem-solving heroes. True, we were not always sitting in our rooms like angels according to admins' expectations. What we were 'out and about' doing, however, was creating real-life/real-world language-learning opportunities and practical applications of that learning. We wanted to share our foreign language teaching and learning strategies with professional colleagues around the city, county, and state—that message being this: Take a risk; step out of your comfort zone; and you, too, can be a Chihuahua Bat.

To that end, an opportunity unexpectedly dropped in our laps one afternoon after school when our district's curriculum specialist, Karen, stopped by Room 13. She asked Mala and me to present a workshop for foreign language teachers in the South Texas region. A local high school in another district, as Karen explained, would be hosting the workshop for teachers to earn continuing education credit. While Karen still was uncomfortable with our approach to teaching a foreign language (but she had to tolerate us because our enrollment increased each year and the parents loved us); while she still was made nervous by the creative style of our class activities; while she still found our immersion projects incomprehensible and our students messy and noisy as they went about their hands-on learning, Karen still needed us and, therefore, asked us to develop a presentation for this workshop.

"Is there any money involved in the presentation, Karen, or is this going to be another freebie?"

"Please, Jean, just look at the proposal before saying no, okay?"

"Well, I guess that answers my gratis question."

"She's kidding." I reached for the proposal in Karen's hand. "Of course, we will look at it." While I had Karen as my captive audience, I said, "Hey, my kids are doing scavenger hunts tomorrow. Can I use your office in which to hide a clue, Karen?"

"No. Tomorrow, I have a meeting; maybe some other time. Let me know about the presentation." With that, Karen spun on her heels and was gone from sight.

"Well, alrighty, then." Looking at Mala, I said, "You know she doesn't get us, right?"

"Here, hand it over," Mala said. "Let me see the proposal form. Hmmm, first line asks for title of the proposed presentation. What if, in our title, we somehow use the phrase, 'Chihuahua Bats' to capture attention?"

"You know Karen won't like that, don't you?"

"Yep. That's why I like it."

The next day, Mala and I took the completed proposal form to the admin office and met with Karen. She expressed surprise that we were so agreeable. "That was easy. What gives?"

"Really, Karen, don't you have any faith in us?" Mala joked.

Karen audibly sighed. "Okay, let's hear it. What's your proposed topic and theme?"

Mala answered. "We have a great title: 'Batting a 1000 with the Chihuahua Bats.' What do you think?"

"I don't like it. It's not very professional. Do you have anything else, such as 'The North Gate Foreign Language Pedagogy'—or something such as that?"

"We brainstormed to come up with this one, Karen. Elizabeth and I like it. We think it's catchy and fun and serves as an immediate attention-grabber. Elizabeth and I both wanted something that will get 'em in the door and get 'em excited about teaching foreign language."

"That's all well and good, but 'Chihuahua Bats' sounds like a joke. You two won't be taken seriously, and you will definitely embarrass North Gate."

The more Karen belittled our proposed title, the more we liked it. However, Karen wouldn't budge from her opinion and refused to fax the form until and unless we agreed to change the title to her idea—'North Gate Foreign Language Pedagogy.' *Yuk. Gag me with a spoon.*

Disappointed, Mala and I returned to Room 13. Determined to find a way around this title controversy, I suddenly had an idea. "What if I take the form home and ask my husband to fax it from his office?"

"I think that just might work," said Mala.

"How mad will the administration get if I do that?"

"That's not important. You just get Mike to fax it for us, and leave the admins to me." I did just that, and Mike got it faxed the next morning right before the deadline.

At the South Texas Regional Teachers of Foreign Languages Workshop, we not only used our Chihuahua Bat title, but we also came up with other related ideas. For example, we thought of providing treats and snacks—calling them 'Bat Bites'—to those who attended our presentation. Our handouts we'd be giving to those teachers? Why, we called those 'Bat Packs.' Our 'Bat Point' power point presentation was so funny that we received a standing ovation! After two long hours, we sat down and gave each other a high five. We did it—one workshop presentation done, and done well—what a notch on our belts!

As Mala and I were catching our breath and trying to come down from our adrenaline rush, a representative from The Texas Foreign Language Association came up to us, introduced herself, and asked about our presentation.

"Are you two the famous Chihuahua Bats I've been hearing about?"

"I don't know about the famous part, but we do claim the name Chihuahua Bat part," I said.

"Well, I was wondering if you two Chihuahua Bats would consider presenting at the Texas Foreign Language Association's fall conference? We always scout for presenters from the different regions of Texas. Especially, we look at the participants' evaluations, and yours were perfect. The Chihuahua Bats have brought enthusiasm back to teaching, I think! The Association would like you to present. I would be glad to write a letter on your behalf to your administration in order for them to give you the necessary 'professional day' away from school. A letter of that sort usually helps convince principals and other admins to approve the leave." Mala and I looked at each other and beamed with excitement and pride. "Now, our Association's fall convention is much bigger than this South Texas regional one; therefore, you would need two different presentations."

"Would you mind sending the request to Francine Davis, our assistant principal, and Mr. James, our Principal at North Gate?" I asked.

"Not at all. I just need the official names and addresses. If you will drop that off at the registration kiosk, under my name (she handed me her business card), I will make sure your administration receives the information and, most important, our endorsement of you two. Good job, Chihuahua Bats! See you in the fall."

"Pinch me," Mala said after she left us. "Did she just say that she liked us?" We were amazed. We were excited. North Gate had barely tolerated Mala's and my teaching strategies over the past three years, but probably only because they didn't really understand them or us. State-mandated testing had their attention, as did the district's ranking as regards students' scores. Consequently, they never really had the time to explore our philosophy. The Foreign Language Association, on the other hand, couldn't praise us enough.

"Well, I guess it's official. We are the Chihuahua Bats," said Mala. "Can you believe it?"

"I know. Go figure. Oh, wow! Now, Mala, we need to get ourselves a shirt with a logo, don't ya think? Holy smokes, We are the—Chihuahua Bats!"

The invitation to be co-presenters at the Texas Foreign Language Association's fall conference was gold to us. That was the validation and the motivation that we needed to continue developing our 'Chihuahua Bat Language Philosophy.'

We didn't have time during the school day to work on our presentations, so we met on Saturdays at Mala's house for the rest of that spring semester of my third year at North Gate. That summer, we got together often to continue our preparations for the big fall workshop. Mala had converted her laundry room into our so-called Bat Office. Every Saturday morning (in-between wash cycles, checkbook questions from Bob, Mala's husband, and playing with "Emmy Lou" and "Reba," Mala's two cute weenie dogs), we cranked out our material. We were a success at the Texas Foreign Language Association's Fall Conference, as well—another notch on our belts.

Furthermore, we worked in our cramped Bat Office in future years, as we were invited to be presenters for even more workshops for teachers of foreign languages. The Chihuahua Bat workshop presentations grew from one per year to four per year; moreover, we wrote and published several books. To illustrate, one of our most-loved publications was *Pigs Can Fly When You Create Language with the Chihuahua Bats*. This book was filled with immersion activities for all levels of language learners. TEKS and TAKS had become the new validation system for public education. With each activity, we created a corresponding assignment template that spoke to all stakeholders. We had done the thinking for the teachers; we had diversified all the activities. As a result, our trademark Chihuahua Bats name and philosophy caught on like wildfire. With that came respect for authentic language-learning. With that, also, came the birth of our company, Chihuahua Bats Language Consultants. No matter what material we presented over the next few years at foreign language workshops, our teacher-participants were always curious about 'Chihuahua Bats'—our crazy name. Honestly, Mala and I had no intelligent reason for the name other than it originated from the goofy mis-reading mistake (due to

Mala's bifocal blindness) of a wrinkled t-shirt logo in Laredo worn by a lying-down librarian!

What is a Chihuahua Bat? Our answer: An educator with a passion for teaching; an educator who dares to go beyond the textbook and teach students to love learning. We each held a strong desire to share our successes with other foreign language teachers and to inspire them to inspire their own students.

We knew that our next challenge was to develop even more authentic immersion activities. How does one do that? By immersing oneself 'in country,' just as we had known was necessary to do with and for our own Spanish students. To be effective in the foreign language classroom, the teacher of that foreign language must and should walk in the footsteps of those one is trying to teach. That leads to another question: What happens when two Chihuahua Bats become language students in Cuernavaca, Mexico?

ELEVEN

Cuernavaca Serenades

Our colleagues were convinced that we were absolutely crazy to teach all year and then fly to another country and teach during the summer, as well. For us Chihuahua Bats, however, Cuernavaca was our salvation—a place to renew our souls and rekindle our childlike enthusiasm. Our passion for the Spanish language and for authentic teaching contributed to our success as educators, we knew, but living 'in country' would nurture our love for and enrich our appreciation of the Mexican language and culture. Doing so also provided Mala and me fresh ideas to incorporate into our classes at North Gate High School.

Little did we know that Cuernavaca would become our Mexican home away from home. Cuernavaca is the capital of the Mexican state of Morelos in what is known as the Valley of Morelos. It is a city of 365,000 (819,000 in its greater metropolitan area) located about an hour south of Mexico City. Known as the City of Eternal Spring, Cuernavaca enjoys weather at a typical seventy degrees and with an abundance of sunshine.

Many wealthy Mexicans own summer homes there. Whenever the state or national economy is not on an upswing, these wealthy Mexicans will rent their homes to foreigners who enroll to study for any length of time at one of the local language schools in the city and surrounding area.

Cuernavaca has twenty-five language schools which attract numerous tourists from around the world. (Over the course of the next five summers when Mala and I lived, studied, and volunteered there, running into other Americans who had also come to study and enjoy the City of Eternal Spring was a common occurrence.) It was just far enough from the pollution and congestion of Mexico City, yet close enough for sight-seeing at all the historical buildings, museums, and monuments.

El Instituto of Cuernavaca was one such language school whose mission statement was to offer a language-immersion experience to students from around the world. Most were from the United States, and most were college students looking for a fast-track to gain Spanish credit on their transcript. This program allowed students to live in a Spanish-speaking environment, forcing them to use only Spanish—or as one might say, to 'live the language.'

The professors, Mexican Nationals, knew just enough English to passingly communicate with those of us from the United States. We students were never allowed to speak English at the school, by the way; that would have been considered disrespectful and inappropriate.

Adult students could enroll by the week, staying to study only that long, or they could enroll for any length of time, extending that, as needed. Instruction, Monday through Friday, was comprised of twenty hours per week. The school days began at 9:00 a.m. and lasted until 1:00 p.m. In the afternoons from 1:30-2:30 p.m., the school offered cultural classes, such as weaving or bark painting or cooking; otherwise, students could sign up for extra practice in conversation or grammar. By 3:00 p.m., everyone—students and professors alike—was home enjoying la comida, the main meal of the day. That, of course, was followed by a siesta to avoid the hottest part of the afternoon.

Mala's and my adventures of living and studying in Cuernavaca began as guests of La Familia Romero, specifically, Señora Romero. She stood five feet two inches tall with short-cropped silver hair highlighted by her original charcoal roots. In her day, she must have been a tiny porcelain doll, but the years and childbirth had added pounds, and now she had a nice, round, grand-motherly figure.

Despite her 'soft' physical appearance, she was a strong woman who had, out of necessity, hardened over the years. Señor Romero had died of a heart attack induced by diabetes in 1965. Because she needed to tend to her home as a widow with five daughters to raise and with no income from a husband, the Señora (as was the case for many other señoras in her neighborhood) went to work for El Instituto, teaching class during the day and providing room and board for students in her home by night.

Aging, she eventually had quit teaching in 1985. By that time, only Rosie (her youngest) remained living in the house with her. Traditionally, the duty of caring for aging parents until their death fell to a family's youngest daugh-ter, should they have one (if not, then such an obligation fell upon either the youngest son or upon another blood relative). This meant that Rosie had never left home since the day she was born. By the time that Mala and I met Señora Romero, her health was in decline. With her other four daughters gone from the home, however, and needing to replace the income she had lost from teaching part-time at El Instituto, the Señora had even more rooms to rent to 'select' students.

Only mature adult students serious about their studies were allowed to room with Señora. She interviewed each one so as to ascertain that prerequisite. She was especially fond of teachers who came to Cuernavaca to matriculate at one of the area's language schools. That is how and why Mala and I—the Chihuahua Bats—met Señora Romero in the summer of 1996 and were counted—as she considered us—among her elite house guests who paid for the privilege of sharing life with her in her home.

At the end of long school years at North Gate, we would return to Cuernavaca as visiting students for a total of five summers. During that time, Señora 'adopted' Mala and me as her American daughters. This was a wonderful compliment. With it came a responsibility that we eagerly accepted. For example, if a grandchild of the Senora's came to visit and was short on money, the family members were each expected to help; as Mala and I were considered family members, Mala and I chipped in our contributions. Birthday gifts from us to the Señora and her blood relatives were greatly appreciated, too.

Mala and I both relished and treasured our time spent with the Señora. With her, we savored long conversations over dinner. Evenings with the Señora were spent sitting beside her on her red velvet sofa—a rather new acquisition of hers and one which she proudly showed off, it often being the center of conversational focus and attention. We watched with her the famous novelas or television soap operas that were her favorites. Over the course of five years of summers, Mala and I became not mere guests in a hotel, but la familia— integral members of the Señora's family. In fact, one precious memory is that when Mala and I would leave for school each morning, Señora would speak a blessing over us both just as if we were her own daughters... and we were.

For the five summers that Cuernavaca and Casa de Romero was our home, Mala and I would awake every morning at 6:00 a.m. to the reliable crowing of Don Beto's rooster. *Once again, I am dealing with a rooster.* Monday through Friday we were thankful for the rooster's irritating persistence, as he was our natural alarm clock, but come Saturday morning, we cursed his reliability and hoped for a nice chicken dinner.

Slowly the neighbors would awake from a peaceful sleep and begin a new day. Each household had distinct noises that would blend together and become a neighborhood symphony.

Often, the cacophony began with the pat-pat-pat of the masa in Margarita's hands, Margarita de Casa de Pedro. "¡Mijas, es la hora de comer!" La madre was calling her girls to come to the table to eat which, in turn, made Mala and me hungry for our own breakfast.

The next movement in the neighborhood symphony came from the swish-swish sweeping sound of the palm frond broom in Señora Sofia's hands as she swept el patio de Casa de Sofia. She was an elderly woman who lived only with her husband; they had had no children. "Viejo, ayúdame, por favor." To translate, Sofia was hollering to her rather reclusive husband by saying 'come and help me, old man.' Señora Sofia, a sociably gregarious woman, probably relished starting her day outside on her porch where she might encounter and interact with others as they roused from their own night's sleep.

Rounding out the morning's choric strains were the melodic songs of the paraquitos in Casa de Don Francisco. "¡Qué bonitos pajaritos, bonitos pajaritos!" Tía Soledad, sister to Don Francisco, would sing her own praises of her pretty parakeets.

Interestingly, Mala and I would take note of when any one household broke from their morning routine. Typically, though, these were the musical routines to which we became accustomed over the course of our five Cuernavaca summers—these and Don Beto's crowing rooster, of course.

We learned to listen for the 6:30 a.m. call of the street vendedor, Marcelino. "Tor-tiiiiiii-llas! Tor-tiiiiii—llas!" That was the signal for either Mala or me to grab three pesos and meet Marcelino (or chase him down) as he cycled throughout the neighborhood streets. Marcelino carried fresh homemade tortillas in the basket mounted on the front of his orange bicycle.

The Señora Romero was insistent on fresh tortillas and fresh squeezed orange juice to start the day. Breakfast was from 7:00-8:00 a.m. and, for us, it would consist of tea, juice, toast, and fruta fresca. The Señora's favorite fruit was mangos and it was at her table where we learned to love mangos and also how to chupa los huesos, literally to eat the entire mango and then suck on the seed for the last bit of juice.

She was also insistent about proper dress code and conversation at her table. One had to be dressed for the day, appropriate for outside the home. House guests had to wear shirts, shorts or pants, and shoes—no sleepwear, not even covered by robes, and certainly no caftans or other such loungewear were permitted at her table. Conversation was always appropriate and in Spanish as the Señora did not speak English.

The seating order was nonnegotiable, too. Señora always sat at the head of the table nearest the kitchen. Rosie, her youngest daughter, was to her left. Any men joining the group would sit at the opposite end of the table. Mala and I were allowed to occupy any of the other five available seats.

Because Señora Romero's health was in decline due to diabetes, she required a housekeeper, Micahela, to help her with the daily chores of the home's interior. One of our favorite parts of the day occurred each breakfast morning—hearing the Señora call for her medicine. She had a unique way of drawing out the syllables of her housekeeper's name. "Micah-eeeeeee-la!" For example, she would holler from the breakfast table, loud enough for all to hear upstairs, for her morning medicines to be brought to her. "Dame mi medicina, Micah-eeeeeee-la!"

Within seconds, we would hear "Voy!" (meaning, 'I am going'). A tiny indigenous woman of not more than four feet eight inches, covered head-to-toe in bedding and with sweat already beading on her brow, would slow-ly descend the stairs and quickly tend to the Señora's medicine. Never missing a step or uttering a word, Micahela would stop her ongoing chores and deliver the medicine, on a silver tray, to Señora.

The funny part was the medicine was always no more than an arm's length behind the Señora on her hutch, but it was Micahela's job to hand it to her. Once Mala and I tried to deliver the medicine, feeling sorry for

Micahela, but we were scowled at and quickly put in our place. The Señora lived by a strict code: Everyone was expected to do the functions pertaining to their social class; everyone, so to speak, was expected to stay within their own lane of the various social strata.

Once breakfast ended around 8:30 a.m., Mala and I would say our goodbyes and depart Casa de Romero for El Instituto. That involved a one-mile walk, some of which was uphill—but first, we always enjoyed our trek through the city.

A cool 65-degree morning typically greeted us as we gently closed the gate to Señora's house and started our walk. We were always excited to be students again; to live in country; and to absorb the culture through all five of our senses. Immersion really was the best way to learn a language, and traveling outside the United States had become our 'second language acquisition philosophy.'

As we walked down Constitución (Señora's street), we greeted el carnicero, "¡Buenos Días!"

"Ah, muy buenos días!" shouted El Carnicero, the butcher. "A la escuela?"

"Sí, a la escuela (to school)," we politely answered.

We next waved to Señora Lupita in la farmacia, already concentrating on filling customers' prescriptions, and wished her a good day. "¡Hola, Señora Lupita! Tenga un buen día."

"¡Hola, estudiantes americanas!"

We then would walk around the corner and onto the other streets that led to the big hill—that Mala and I called our mountain—and ultimately to El Instituto. This was the fun part of our walk each weekday morning going to school. The streets were lined with an eclectic mixture of tiendas—little street market stores. Mala and I couldn't help perusing the varieties of toys, candies, baskets, vases, flowers, clothes, hats, shoes, and jewelry. We were always on the look-out for items to take back and use in our classes but catching ourselves if we loitered too long and might be late for our first class of the day.

On such weekly morning excursions as we traversed past the tiendas, Mala and I often would study the vocabulary used to describe promotional items; we'd then compare those colloquial words to the words that were presented in the textbooks. We wanted to absorb everything.

Reaching yet another street corner to round, the pungent aroma of onions and peppers assailed our nostrils.

A local vendor, cooking on his carbon live-fire street grill in front of Tito's panadería or bakery, was responsible for that olfactory experience.

"Ah, Mala said, can you smell it? The grilled onions and peppers outside, and the whole-grained breads, corn and wheat tortillas, and pastries inside!"

Before we could even step foot inside the door of Tito's Bakery, we heard, "¡Maestras, muy buenos días, dos amigas!" It was Mariana, the baker's daughter.

"Hola," I said in return to Mariana.

Just looking at and smelling all the new pastries and cakes was sufficient enough to fill anyone with delight. As I meandered, surveying the counters, I enjoyed the sounds of Tito kneading bread. I loved watching the rhythm of his hands as he deftly handled the dough back and forth. Holding the dough up to his ear (much as one might hold up a conch shell to the ear as if listening for sounds of the ocean), Tito would listen intently, as if the dough were really talking to him. With a wink, he would declare, "My secret is listening to the bread."

Tito had inherited the bakery from his parents; it had been in his family for four generations. Mariana, his daughter, had dreams of graduating high school and going to university in Mexico City, but Tito insisted to his daughter that she must obey tradition and carry on the family business. This explained Mariana's occasional melancholy moods and her search for a rich American to take her away from her father's world. This also explained her thrill at seeing us, the teachers from Los Estados Unidos, walk into her father's bakery each summer morning. Mala and I represented her dream of escape.

"What do you think? Pan dulce to dip in our coffee?

"Yes, pan dulce with the pink sugar," said Mala as she walked over to the bottled waters and grabbed two. "I'll get the water, and you get the sweet bread. Meet you outside." Mala would then approach the check-out counter.

"Mariana, dos aguas, por favor."

"Dos aquas, un peso cincuenta, y un hombre muy rico (translated as 'two waters, one dollar fifty, plus a rich man')," Mariana would always say back to Mala.

"Now, Mariana, you know that I can't fit a rich guy in my pocket. Besides," Mala would say to her friend the baker's daughter, "just maybe I am keeping the rich man for my siesta this afternoon."

Mariana would always give Mala her laughter in return.

"Okay, mañana, maybe you have deeper pockets, eh?"

Mala would flash Mariana a playful smile as she paid for the water. Exiting the panadería, we both waved goodbye, often just in time to cross the street when the traffic light changed from red to green.

Then, looming in front of us, was the big hill, our mountain to climb. El Instituto and our future destiny as the Chihuahua Bats team would be found at its apex. Mala and I had to climb that peak each morning in order to reach the summit.

TWELVE

The Path, the Passion, the Pinnacle

Vividly, I recall the first time that Mala and I trekked our way up to El Instituto. What the native population of Cuernavaca saw as a hill—albeit, a big hill—Mala and I (we from the plains of South Texas) saw as a mountain. On that first journey to our Spanish language immersion school, I remember saying, "Are you ready to huff and puff and high-foot it up to El Instituto? These first few days are gonna be the hardest," I said, "since we Texans are used to driving our cars everywhere we go."

"Whew!" Mala huffed. I'll be glad—when—we are in— better shape—from all our—walking—we're gonna be—doing this summer." Mala gave reply, despite her already gulping for air.

"Me, too," I said, grabbing my own big gulp of air to try and relieve my burning leg muscles that were screaming for more oxygen.

Cuernavaca sits at an elevation of about 5,000 feet above sea level (1,500 meters). This may be compared to the elevation of our South Texas area's altitude of a mere 787 feet above sea level. No wonder our lungs were not acclimated to our new environment. We inevitably and by destiny, though, would reach our Spanish language school. For five consecutive summers, we did so—climbing that 'mountain,' both physically and metaphorically.

For our first summer, El Instituto was celebrating its twenty-fifth year of operation. Again, my memories of the place remain vivid. One might describe its campus as aesthetically pleasing, relaxing, functional, and interesting. The rooms were all hand painted with murals from the local artisans. Each classroom was named after a famous person in Mexico's history. For example, two classrooms—Salon Rivera and Salon Kahlo—were named after Mexican artists Diego Rivera and Frida Kahlo. A guard always stood attentively at the entrance gate to assist students. A tropical paradise with grass hut palapas, palm trees, waterfalls, and stone carved statues greeted those who entered. Just outside the offices were a lobby and gift shop. Behind the office

was a courtyard that opened onto a beautifully land-
scaped yard with a pool and snack bar. All the classes
either faced the courtyard or the pool area. Studying
at El Instituto was relaxing and peaceful. School began
at 9:10 a.m., with a break at 11:00 a.m., and then ended
at 1:00 p.m. Students' afternoons were free for excursions, extra language instruction, or participating in the
outreach programs sponsored by El Instituto.

Generally arriving by 9:00 a.m. gave Mala and me just
enough time to grab a cup of coffee at the snack bar and
be seated before the professor arrived to begin the first
class of the day. We came to refer to him as 'Estimado
Profesor' (meaning, 'dear' and 'esteemed' and 'well-re-
garded' teacher). Pleasing him was important to Mala
and me because we were his favorite students—not
due to our impressive brilliance but to our passion for
teaching and embracing the Spanish language and culture. That is what drew recognition to us. Moreover,
our charismatic and comedic personalities brought life
to the typically serious classroom instruction.

By 9:07 a.m., Mala and I were entering the classroom.
On one of the hand-painted trays that we had purchased at el mercado during some prior summer, she
and I would neatly set the bakery sweet breads that we
had bought at Tito's Panadería—the pan dulce—and a
cup of coffee, and then place the tray on Profe's small

table beside his desk. The other international language students would watch with curiosity.

Generally, I would make remarks to them, such as the following. "Trust us, coffee and sweet breads for Estimado Profesor always enhances the lesson! By the way, I would introduce myself, "you can call me Swan, and this is my friend—you can call her Mala. Back at the high school where we teach in Texas, we are known together as the 'Chihuahua Bats,' so you could call us that, too—or even just 'Bats,' for short." I would then typically ask the other international students in our class, "Have you ever studied at El Instituto before?" Each would introduce themselves to Mala and me, as well as speak briefly of their foreign language involvement and experience. Each summer, all were Spanish teachers, and all were first-timers at El Instituto.

Other first-timers in our class would tend to ask Mala and me what kind of class this would be or what is the teacher like or will the instructor teach from the textbook. We would typically answer by telling them that for some days, we won't even open our textbook. We'd explain that Profe is kind enough to talk about real aspects of Mexican culture—aspects that aren't found in a textbook. We'd add that one can always read the chapters on his or her own, saying that a professor is not needed for what we can do for ourselves.

After such small talk, a silence would fall. The class would wait with anticipation for Estimado Profesor Emilio Dalí. Mala and I would listen for the familiar footsteps. Profesor would walk into class, usually clearing his throat perhaps to get our attention, and with perhaps an air of arrogance. He would always dress quite neatly in slacks; a long-sleeved, button-down shirt; a tie; and a sweater vest. Tall, slender, and with distinguished-looking silver hair, Profesor Emilio carried himself with and exuded pride and sophistication. He held four degrees—all in the field of literature—and was known to brag often about his Estudios Peninsulares (studies in Spanish literature at various universities in Spain). To explain that term, in the context of the Spanish colonial caste system, a 'peninsular' was or is a Spaniard whose birth and/or heritage may be directly connected to the peninsula of Spain. The peninsulares were and are a special group at the pinnacle of that caste system interwoven with ethnicity, class, and race. A hint of superiority among those educated in Spain was lorded over those educated in Mexico, Mala and I observed. The esteemed Profesor Emilio Dalí had joined the staff of El Instituto five years prior, and for that number of summer seasons, Mala and I were privileged to study under him.

Another privilege—and passion—of ours was to volunteer in our spare time with the service programs in the community sponsored by El Instituto. This institution had the vision and the mission to help the less fortunate citizens of Cuernavaca, many of whom had never attended school because they were busy scrounging for a living by walking the streets selling souvenirs to tourists. Although many visiting language students only took advantage of the language instruction, Mala and I believed language classes alone would not totally immerse us into all aspects of the culture. For that, becoming part of the community and its various volunteer programs supported Mala's and my cultural-immersion goal. We were especially excited about the educational programs through Outreach, a non-profit organization that provided education for the poor.

On one occasion during our fifth summer studying and volunteering in Cuernavaca, Mala and I heard a familiar voice coming from behind us. "Bat girls? Where have you been? I missed you at orientation last night!" said Sandi, the Director of Recruiting for El Instituto. Spanish was not her first language, but she had mastered enough to communicate effectively. Sandi was a fun personality, but she was also a wheeler dealer. To explain, Sandi often would host dinner parties and invite the students whom she thought would help her agenda of increasing enrollment at El Instituto.

"That has to be you, Sandi. A day without Sandi is a day without drama," said Mala.

"All right, don't start with me!"

"Sandi, good to see you," I said. Anticipating more banter between Mala and her, I quickly interjected my question: "What project do have for us this year?"

Sandi had been the program director of El Instituto for five years. She was on staff at the University of Michigan; she had come in person to visit the Cuernavaca language school before allowing her university students to attend for credit. She fell in love with Cuernavaca and El Instituto and was offered an 'in country' recruiting position with the school. She returned home to Michigan, packed up, and moved her family to Cuernavaca. Her passion for educating was awakened to a new level, and she followed her passion.

"Project? Can't I just be glad to see you two? Okay, okay, you know me too well! I do have a proposition for the crazy Chihuahua Bats."

"So, what is this project?" I asked. After the past several years, the administrators at El Instituto had come to rely on Mala and me to help with teacher recruitment for their community outreach programs. Our Spanish skills and enthusiastic personalities meshed well with first-time teachers in country. El Instituto would compensate us by reducing our tuition fees. They even put some of our Chihuahua Bat publications—produced by our company, Chihuahua Bats Language Consultants—in their book store.

"Swan, let me get these students on the bus for an excursion. Can I entice you two to join me at Café Universal at about five today? We can talk about this opportunity that I think you will enjoy."

"Sure, Sandi, see you at 5:00 p.m. sharp," I said.

Looking at our afternoon schedule, Mala and I realized that at 2:30 p.m., we had just enough time to leave school, stop at Casa Maria to buy a Coca Cola to have with our food (many of Senora's neighbors sold sundry little items out of their homes to make ends meet), and enjoy la comida at 3:00 p.m. with Señora before meeting Sandi two hours later.

"¡Hola, Hola!" Mala and I heard her familiar voice of greeting from where she waited for us on her balcony. We hollered and waved back at Señora.

La comida was an important part of the Mexican culture and the best part of the day. We were never surprised to see a friend or a relative joining us. A leisurely two-to-three-hour lunch, comida involved family and fellowship, with everyone at table relishing discussions about the topics of the day—whether that was something Mala and I had just learned at El Instituto;

comparing our two cultures; or what all was happening anywhere politically, such as a certain U.S. President's dalliances in the Oval Office.

As this particular enjoyable meal came to a close, the hands on my watch prompted me to announce, "Señora, it's time for your story! We don't want you to miss your 'El Amor Gitano' (Gypsy Love), do we?"

"¡Micah, tráeme más café! Amiguitas, al sofá, por favor. ¡Ándales!" (Bring me more coffee. Ladies to the sofa. Hurry!) Every weekday, we watched Señora's favorite novelas sitting on her red velvet sofa. She loved to engage with the plot and give the melodramatic characters a piece of her mind, and Mala and I loved watching her as we sat on either side of her. We used this activity as a way to improve our listening comprehension. The segment on this day was a particularly juicy segment of "El Amor Gitano" because 'El Gitano' was being kidnapped and taken to jail. If he wanted to pursue his true love, he would have to escape the narrow confines that held him trapped. *Don't we all?*

Now, suddenly noticing the time on the clock was Mala's turn. "Señora, we have to meet Sandi this afternoon. La comida was excellent, as always. Will you excuse us, please?"

"Bueno, maestras—but por favor, be very careful. Just

last week, a robbery occurred in the mercado. Tourists were approached and surrounded by some venders. You know they like to distract you and then, while you are looking one way, they take your backpack."

"We will be careful, Señora. Don't worry."

We flagged a taxi and arrived outside of Café Universal on time and with a few minutes to spare. Surrounding this café and others could always be found indigenous people, including their children as young as three years old, who worked as street vendors peddling their wares daily in a small mercado across from the zócalo or square. They would walk the streets fourteen to fifteen hours a day hawking their products to tourists. Frowned upon by the café owners, the street vendors also would saunter through their establishments—a veritable harvest field of tourists to whom they could sell their wares. Mala and I enjoyed talking with each one and had become friends over the past several summers with a few. Each summer, our tradition was to visit each booth; buy personal souvenirs; and then place orders for souvenirs that were promised to friends and family back home. The artisan peddlers did well enough during the summer months when tourism was high, but then, many would barely survive until March when spring break brought more tourists. Our buying extra from the street sellers was really to help them make it until spring.

The children of the vendors found a special place in our hearts. Running up and hugging us or tugging on our shirts, they always captured our attention. Mala and I would form a circle with them and play games like "Pato, Pato, Ganso" (Duck, Duck, Goose) or "Simón Dice" (Simon Says) until we heard an irritated parent call to their child, "¡Mijo, Mija! ¡Vende, no juegues!" (My child! Go sell, do not play). The Bats found it hard not to play with the children, los niños, as we browsed and shopped in the mercado.

One could spend afternoons watching the world go by while enjoying a Coca Cola at Café Universal. With circulating Casablanca ceiling fans and brightly-colored pink and green floral cushions on the chairs, Café Universal was our escape for an hour every evening. Into this, our favorite café in Cuernavaca, Mala and I entered. There was Sandi waving us over to her table. We joined her; she wasted no time in presenting her project.

"So, Chihuahua Bats, I want to explain a new Outreach project. You have been such a success working with our indigenous children in several of our programs sponsored by El Instituto. We have recently opened a new school, and we need your help."

"A new school. Tell us more," said Mala.

"As you both are aware, El Instituto's outreach programs empower youth by providing a free education for the children of the indigenous poor, such as those we can see now outside the window of this cafe. During siesta, as you surely have come to learn, many vendors allow their children to stop selling and attend one of our outreach schools, but only for that brief amount of late-afternoon siesta time.

"We secured a property about two months ago. It's an old cinder block building in one of the area's poorest population groups. *Oh no! More cinder blocks.* The school is located in Civac, just on the outskirts of Cuernavaca. I need you to understand that Civac is quite, quite remote. To get there is not an easy journey."

"Some of our first-timer students at El Instituto helped us clean it—we would have loved to give the walls fresh paint, but we lack funds for doing that. Some of El Instituto's maintenance crew managed to deliver some folding tables and a number of chairs. We don't even have one portable blackboard, unfortunately." *Ah, yes, I remember the days of no blackboard in my old North Gate industrial tech room.*

"We have been so grateful for our initial volunteers— our cleaning crew—and the few staff members from El Instituto temporarily assisting them. Other than those people, I did manage to recruit several teacher volunteers, and we were able to open the doors of Escuelita to any children whose parents would allow them to attend during the siesta hours. We've been open about a month, now—only on Tuesdays and Thursdays—and our enrollment is swelling each week. At this point, Escuelita is basically just an old building—but a building that already has an enrollment on any given Tuesday or Thursday of from sixty-five to ninety-five children and youth. Our few volunteer teachers are overworked, to say the least; I'm worried they will quit on us and leave the program."

"Thus, we are in need of more volunteer teachers and, again, in dire need of school supplies. I was hoping The Bats would be willing to volunteer there this summer? (Her statement was more of an imploring question.) We need your enthusiasm. The few teacher volunteers who've been with us from the beginning are fatigued, frustrated, and frankly—uninspired. I'm hoping they don't quit before we've barely begun. I've been trying to recruit from our regular pool of teacher volunteers, but many of them are afraid to get too close to these particular children."

That last statement shocked me. "Why?" I wondered aloud.

"I guess they think these children have germs or lice or other parasites or diseases; I also frankly think that some are just afraid that they don't really speak the language well enough." Sandi let out a long sigh. "I don't know. I don't know." Sandi stared at Mala and me, pausing perhaps to allow us to absorb and process all of her information.

"Are you two up for the challenge this summer—and I mean, beginning immediately?

Will you two help?"

Glancing first at Mala, who gave me a wink, I then said, "We would love to help."

"Wonderful! I can't thank you both enough. I must warn you, though," Sandi continued, "the journey to Escuelita is long and rugged. You have to take La Ruta (the local bus line) to Civac, which is a thirty-minute ride. From there, the path to Escuelita is nothing more than a rocky, dirt road; it then will take you to the bottom of a mountain. From the base, you two are going to have an arduous hike up that mountain—and there sits Escuelita, on its pinnacle. Oh! And if you are not on the 6:00 p.m. La Ruta, you two will be spending the night in Civac. The last bus leaves promptly at 6:00 p.m. Are you still in, Chihuahua Bats?"

Mala and I looked at each other again and said in unison, "We are in." After reassuring her, I asked Sandi the name of our contact person for when we arrived.

"Angela," she said. "Angela is our director. She will fill you in on helpful details. Let's see, tomorrow's Thursday. Can you meet her tomorrow after la comida? In fact, can you two Chihuahua Bats just count on tomorrow being your first day of school at Escuelita—specifically, starting at 4:00 p.m.?"

First day. First day. I thought back to my first day at North Gate five years earlier. Five years ago, I had stepped with determination onto a path of intentionality to become the best teacher that I could be—a trajectory—that eventually led me here to Cuernavaca and tomorrow to Escuelita high atop one of the mountains of Mexico. Tomorrow would be a new 'first day'—one that already was filling my cup to the brim with excitement, anticipation, hope, purpose, and passion. *Indeed, my cup runneth over.* I nodded 'yes' for both Mala and me.

"Great! See you Thursday at Escuelita. Don't forget, you will need to bring your own supplies, as we do not have anything but kids right now. I must warn you, so you won't be too shocked—the living conditions are extremely poor."

"Don't worry about that," Mala said. "All we need are the kids."

Mala and I exited Café Universal and headed straight to the mercado to buy supplies. We found new story books for reading to the children; coloring books; tracing paper; map pencils; and some math practice books for the older kids. We also bought a few toys for the children's recreational needs, toys that both the girls and the boys would enjoy. Among those items, Mala and I bought a few soccer balls; we knew these would be a favorite with the kids and something out-of-reach for their poor parents to buy for them. We also purchased some small, bouncy rubber balls; with these, the children would be able to improvise the game of dunking balls into plastic cups, not to mention tossing to one another and/or simply bouncing to one another. What's more, we found a couple of jump ropes and a few packages of colored balloons.

The next day after la comida with the Senora, Mala and I headed out toward the city in order to catch our ride on La Ruta. Our backpacks were laden with supplies and toys. We were excited for our new adventure. Indeed, our entire careers up to this point had prepared each of us for this adventure.

Escuelita, as Sandi had explained to us the evening before at Café Universal, was a bus ride to the outskirts of Cuernavaca. Civac was an industrial suburb of rapid development. Billboards advertised new housing subdivisions and soon-coming businesses. The ride through Civac was typical of many bus rides through any such town in Mexico. Mala sat by the window so that she could breathe in fresh air in the hope of calming her motion sickness, and I sat on the aisle seat holding a small child who could not fit on the seat next to his mother, as she was holding two other of her children. Rutas are older and smaller city buses that carry, on average, twenty-four to thirty passengers. Despite the seats being meant for only two, families would crowd together on them, whether there was room or not. Old, white vehicles without air-conditioning, they were meant to be a quick and inexpensive way to go from one destination to another.

As we arrived at the outer edges of Civac, our paved road sure-enough ended, and La Ruta turned onto a narrow and rocky, dirt road. Bumping along through the poorest sector of the outskirts of Civac, we noticed most all of the buildings were abandoned; some had been taken over by squatters. Housing (if one could call even call it that) consisted of nothing more than a refrigerator box; a large wooden crate from the car factory; or a sheet of plywood that leaned against a partial cinder block wall. Furniture, most or all of which sat in the dirt, were small vegetable crates; hammocks strung between two tree trunks; a tree stump; or just a conveniently placed large rock. Curtains were simply old t-shirts that had been ripped and somehow secured over openings of any given 'house' in order to provide some degree of privacy. A massive mess of electrical wiring looped and drooped and dangled overhead in an obvious display of pirated electricity. Women were cooking on small sheets of metal over campfires while they nursed their babies. Families, gathered together on their improvised furniture, prayed over their meal of tortillas—and only that, tortillas. No bathrooms; no running water—these people were among the poorest of the poor. Silent, Mala and I each drank in this scene of the most abject poverty that either of us had ever seen. *Wow! I just thought I knew what poverty looked like.*

As I watched the to-and-fro activity of their daily routines from my rickety seat on La Ruta, I said to Mala, "We will never have enough money to help these poor people...so many children, so many families in need, what can we do?"

"All we can do is teach them and hope that they will use their knowledge to better themselves, their families, and their community of others."

"You're right. I guess so. That is why we have been called into this field—to teach."

Suddenly, Mala wailed, "Oh, no! Sandi wasn't kidding. That really is a mountain." Mala was shading her eyes from the sun as she looked out her window.

"Wow! We are in for a climb, Mala." La Ruta stopped and the driver reminded us to be back here at 6:00 p.m. or stay the night. He chuckled with that last comment. We filed out of the bus; shaded our eyes from the hot, bright sun; and pointed our gaze straight up to Escuelita perched atop the tall, rugged mountain that loomed before us.

"Okay, Swan, Let's start hiking."

Slowly and strategically, we stepped on rocks and stones that people had placed along the path to help with the climbing, especially the elderly and the children. For every other step, we would have to balance ourselves on a wobbly stone by placing a hand on the ground. Halfway up the mountain, I could see adults carrying plastic lawn chairs and tables into a cinder block building. As the path curved to the left, we could now see a signboard with the words 'Escuelita' above the door. A woman waving her arms jubilantly at us welcomed Mala and me as we finally made it to the door huffing and puffing.

"Angela? Are you Angela?"

"Sí," she said. "¡Bienvenidos!"

"Sandi...wasn't kidding...when she told me that...reaching...Escuelita...would mean climbing...a mountain," I said as I was still trying to catch my breath.

Angela began apologizing for the climb and the minimal surroundings.

"Please, don't worry. All we need is the children," assured Mala.

"Niños, we have lots of niños—eighty-six to ninety children every afternoon, and that's just from this past month of opening Escuelita! We anticipate more because we know from the other outreach schools that parents will usually let their little sellers get off the streets once the selling season is done."

"Please, show us to the children. Mala and I are eager to get started." Setting my backpack on the floor, I opened it up and pulled out some books. I had the sense that this was a precipice moment in my career, in my life.

The children, all different ages, were sitting in a semicircle on the concrete floor. *Like one other classroom concrete floor*, I recalled. Many had their younger and smaller siblings, still wearing diapers, sitting on their laps.

Mala and I divided the kids into two reading groups. Mala took one group, and I took the other. With my group, I began by asking if any of them had a favorite book or story that they wanted to hear. They began offering their favorites until one little girl said the magic words, "Me gustan los perros."

"I'm so glad you like books about dogs because I just happen to have a dog book here to read to you!" The children gleefully clapped their hands. I held it up for my group to see and read the title to them, "*¡Corre, Perro Corre!* (The English version is 'Go, Dog, Go!') Let's start with that one."

"¡Sí, Sí, Señora!" Hands clapped again.

Mala and I each read three books to our respective groups. The children were mesmerized by our animated voices that we used to dramatize the stories, bringing them to life. Not only was this activity great Spanish practice for us, but for the children, as well—many of whom spoke a combination of Nahuatl (referring to the ancient Aztec language) mixed with Spanish. At the end of each story, I knew that Mala would do what I was doing; namely, we would target certain vocabulary, reviewing those particular words by having the children play some sort of a game to reinforce their learning.

After story time, the children had a short recess while

the director prepared a late afternoon meal. One of the benefits of the program was food; for many children, this would be their only meal for the day. We teacher volunteers helped the children form a line to wash their hands before eating. Without running water, the children would rinse their hands in a plastic bucket that contained water and sulfa, and then they would dry their hands on the same towel. What began as a white towel became, by the last child in line, ash gray.

Angela explained to us that since nutrition was a concern, the school had been giving each child a bag of vitamins to take and use at home. Angela had been hearing from the parents, however, that they refused to give their children these vitamins because doing so might increase their appetites, and they couldn't afford to feed the family more than once a day.

"What did you do about that?" I asked.

"We put the vitamins in the juice. That way, their parents don't know."

"That's smart," I said. Glancing at my watch, I noticed the hands showed 5:30 p.m. Mala was talking to a group of children; I signaled her by pointing to my watch.

Picking up on that cue, Angela cleared her throat and instructed the children to say 'gracias' to us, their new teachers. Angela then counted out a rhythmic 'uno-dos-tres' that led to the children singing to us. It was a song that praised God for new friends. Each time they sang the word 'amigas,' the children pointed to Mala and me.

I nudged Mala and whispered, "Wow. They are praising God for us? I am speechless. They are the heroes, not us." Overwhelmed, I felt a knot in my throat.

"I know. Try not to lose it, Swan. If you lose it, then I'll lose it; then, we'll look like a couple of crying idiots." Instead, we clapped and thanked them for such a beautiful song, wishing them well until next Tuesday.

We managed our emotions while making our way back down the mountain. We held our emotions in check until La Ruta pulled away from the base of the mountain. Slowly, the tears began to silently stream down my face. I couldn't find words—if anyone had expected that of me—to describe what had just been an unforgettable mountaintop experience.

Finally, having almost arrived back in Cuernavaca, I found some. "I only thought I knew what poverty meant until I saw that situation, and yet, Mala, those children are so happy. They're so enthusiastic to be at school. I mean, Mala, they live in boxes and crates, for goodness sakes."

"This is all they know, Swan. As they get older, the struggles of living in abject poverty will be a much greater challenge. For now, though, they just enjoy life."

Some scene out the bus's window evidently had caught her attention. Mala looked at me and pointed out her window to a huge pile of dirt where two little boys, maybe three years old, were jumping and sliding down the dirt pile. Giggling, shrieking peals of laughter filled our ears as La Ruta rumbled past them. The tots were covered in dirt from head to toe. *What fun they're having.* I couldn't help but smile, on the outside and the inside of my heart.

Back in Cuernavaca, we didn't have an ounce of energy to walk back to the zócalo. "Taxi sounds good to me. After all we did climb a mountain," I said.

As soon as a taxi rounded the corner, we flagged it and settled into a much more comfortable seat than La Ruta had offered us. We decided that we needed to decompress at Café Universal. Sitting in the hunter green wicker chairs with their bright pink, overstuffed cushions felt great on our backs. The breeze from the oscillating Casablanca fans felt refreshing on our faces. Sipping on cocas, we sank back in our tropical chairs and debriefed our thoughts and feelings from the afternoon of our first day spent with the children of Escuelita.

"Several hours with those kids sure takes it out of us, but it was worth it, wasn't it?" said Mala.

"I know. To me, this is real teaching. No meetings, no committees, no curriculum alignment."

"I agree. It's so rewarding just to teach. What is it that we always say? 'Leave us alone, and just let us teach,' right? This new school program is going to thoroughly renew our teacher-souls, Swan."

"Yes. To be able to work with children who are not mandated to attend school is a real treat, isn't it? Watching the children at Escuelita enjoying with us our first day of school with them was inspiring. Did you notice the difference in those children's expressions this afternoon during story time—as compared with the facial expressions of children forced to sell trinkets on the streets? There is just no comparison."

We visited Escuelita seven more times that summer. Each time, we took more supplies and books for the children to enjoy. On our last Thursday, we gave each child a small gift: We presented each girl with some hair ties and each boy with a small, nerf soccer ball. For one final time, the children thanked us with their song. In turn, Mala and I sang "Jesus Loves the Little Children" for them. The children clapped and hugged us goodbye. How hard it was for us to leave them, knowing that we might not ever see them again.

On our last day there, Angela expressed her gratitude for our willingness to not merely volunteer, but
also that Mala and I had gone above and beyond her
expectations by developing enrichment reading activities for the students, which she so appreciated. Angela
explained that over the years, she had worked with
wonderful volunteers—all with servants' hearts—but,
in her words, very few had been real teachers such as
Mala and I.

Our lively interactions with those children was a mo-
tivating factor in them coming to school on those
Tuesdays and Thursdays; the opportunity for learning
was a gift to each child, and they seemed to feel that.
Likewise, their returning to Escuelita each time was a
precious gift to us. Escuelita, we knew, would always
hold a special place in our hearts.

Riding La Ruta; choking on the dust from the dirt roads;
watching the families in their impoverished homes cope
with their chores of daily life; hiking up the mountain;
and teaching those dear children had changed both of
our lives forever. Before we descended the mountain
for the last time that summer, Mala and I paused on the
summit. From that vantage point, we looked out over
the 'box city' neighborhood and reflected on how far
we had journeyed together as educators and as friends.

During our flight back to Texas that ended our fifth summer as a team in Cuernavaca, I reflected upon my own journey. Looking back now—teaching in that old industrial tech room that jutted up next to that open-ceilinged clinic and sharing it with theatre classes—all of that was nothing compared with the struggles these impoverished Mexican families faced daily. *What was I thinking, complaining about noise and the lack of supplies? I was so ashamed.*

Mala and I had climbed a mountain—physically, mentally, emotionally, and spiritually. For sure, I had learned that not having the ideal classroom or a stockpile of supplies is not what teaching's purpose is. Teaching is about capturing the hearts of students and making a difference in their lives. This goes for students and their teachers found anywhere in the world. Escuelita had taught me that valuable lesson.

"Mala, I will never walk into a classroom and be only a 'textbook teacher,' will you?"

"No."

"Learning a new language is about living that language. We must share our philosophy with our other foreign language colleagues, don't you agree?"

"Yes."

As we soared through a sea of white clouds with glimpses of cobalt blue interspersed with striations of the sun's rays, my mind drifted back to Escuelita once more. I said to my friend and colleague, "Just think, Mala, if it were not for having a school to attend, even just during the two-hours of siesta, those precious children would not eat."

"I know, Swan. It breaks my heart." The airline's Styrofoam coffee cup that Mala held in her hand paused mid-air. A tear rolled down her face.

That one tear spoke volumes to me. That one tear held a world inside it. That one tear was worth at least one book—my memoir telling the story of two teachers who met each other during a telephone interview; who, in tandem, had passionately journeyed on a challenging but rewarding path in pursuit of excellence in teaching; and who, together, had climbed a high mountain as they reached for the pinnacle of their careers.

#

CPSIA information can be obtained
at www.ICGtesting.com
Printed in the USA
BVHW071936121119
563653BV00001B/61/P